Endorsements

"Danny Ray is one-of-a-kind. His illusions will amaze, but what will stand out even more is his authenticity. He doesn't want to just entertain, he wants to leave a lasting, positive impact wherever he goes."

— Brent Squires, Student Ministry Pastor,
Bay Area community church,
Coach at youth ministry institute

"Danny Ray has always been, and continues to be, a steady and solid voice of wisdom in these perilous times. His words have always been anointed by the Lord! This book is a must have if you're married or plan to get married."

— Michael Thompson,
Lead Pastor, Gospel Community Church

"For anyone who seems to feel that much of the magic has seeped out of their marriage, this collection of wise and remarkably practical tips from a master Magician will be just what is needed to bring back the "oohs" and "ahhs" of delight into their relationship."

— Rick Bundschuh, Pastor,
Cartoonist, author of *Soul Surfer*, Kauai, Hawaii

"This book should be a must read for any couple considering the lifelong commitment of marriage. Fun for a couple to read together,

Danny uses humor along with tricks and tips which makes them easy to apply yet challenges a couple to grow and implement change. He points out the need for Jesus to be in the center of our relationship which is needed in today's world of 'all about me' mentality."

— Gail Wiles,
Church Equipping Director, Grace Bomb

"After being in ministry for 25 years, I've become a little skeptical when I hear about new books, on almost any topic, that are supposed to have a significant impact on people. Sometimes, the hype is just too much, and sometimes, the book just doesn't deliver. *No, I Can't Make Your Wife Disappear* isn't one of those books and believe me when I tell you—it delivers!

"If you are looking for a fresh take on marriage books, practical wisdom delivered in an engaging and often entertaining way, and an author who has lived out what they are writing, then this is your book! Danny and Kimberly bring a unique perspective gained from over two decades of life on the road. They are real about their own struggles, they aren't afraid to talk about difficult topics, and they challenge the reader to take steps toward making their own marriages great. This is a book worth your time."

— Joe Castaneda,
Founder of Overboard Ministries

"Right away when we first discussed this project, I could clearly see that Danny's heart ached to help strengthen marriages. I LOVE how he and Kimberly have worked together—much like a successful marriage—to hone this message into a powerful and entertaining book that will change your life! That's no illusion!"

— Jim House,
Owner, The Book Carver

"I have watched Danny perform mind-blowing magic for years, and now he has written a mind-blowing book on marriage! This book is packed full of practical ways to bring the magic back into your marriage! It's fun to read and hard to put down. Danny has saved his best magic for making an entertaining and honest book that will improve your marriage in every way.

"This book is full of wisdom, communicated with clarity and aims at application. I cannot recommend this book highly enough. It's destined to become a classic!"

— Dr. Rod Collins,
Lead Pastor, Sanctuary Church

NO, I CAN'T MAKE YOUR WIFE DISAPPEAR

NO, I CAN'T MAKE YOUR WIFE DISAPPEAR

A MAGICIAN'S GUIDE FOR A ***MAGICAL MARRIAGE***

DANNY RAY

Birmingham, Alabama

No, I Can't Make Your Wife Disappear: A Magician's Guide to a Magical Marriage

Iron Stream Media
100 Missionary Ridge
Birmingham, AL 35242
IronStreamMedia.com

Iron Stream Media serves its authors as they express their views, which may not express the views of the publisher.

Library of Congress Control Number: 2021945749

ISBN: 978-1-56309-554-2 paperback
ISBN: 978-1-56309-555-9 ebook

1 2 3 4 5—25 24 23 22 21
Printed in the United States of America

Dedication

Kimberly,
You are the love of my life.
You are my best friend.
You are my dream come true.
You simply are my magic.

Contents

ACKNOWLEDGMENTS

The process for creating magic often happens alone. I sit by myself in my study, out on the patio, or even in a coffee shop, working on a trick or trying to develop a new over-the-top effect. Only after months and sometimes years of rehearsal do I let other people view the work in progress and then I continue to refine moves until I think the illusion is ready for the stage.

Books are something else altogether.

This book is in your hands today because a team of people supported my wife, Kimberly, and me throughout the writing process. I once heard a publisher say that everyone has a book inside of them but not everyone has a team to help them produce it.

Jim House spent an entire day with me that really helped all my ideas formulate.

Gretchen Hicks has reviewed every word of this document and has improved it in every way. She has also done a tremendous job of keeping me on track through the writing process to make sure deadlines were met while not failing in the other facets of our ministry.

Joe Castaneda has carried this project through the ups and downs. He has inspired me, encouraged me, and challenged me to write to change lives.

Chip MacGregor has been far more than a literary agent. Thank you for your constant encouragement to bring this project to life. Thank you for believing in it from the very beginning.

The team at Iron Stream Media has been unbelievably supportive, and their creative insights into this project are impossible to enumerate. Thank you, Suzanne Kuhn, for your prayers, Larry J. Leech II for your refining and polishing the book, Linda Gilden and Denise Loock for challenging me, and the entire team that includes Bradley Isbell, Kim McCulla, and Lori Lenz-Heiselman. Words cannot express my gratitude. You all are amazing.

Thank you to author, speaker, pastor, and friend Rick Bundschuh for reading the early manuscript and encouraging me to push this project to the finish line.

Thank you to everyone who read early manuscripts—offering insights, giving critiques, and supporting Kimberly and me every step of the way.

And of course, none of this would be written without the last twenty-five years of marriage to Kimberly. You are the woman of my dreams. Your insights are woven into every page of this book. Without your grace in my life and dedication to this project, this book never would have come to life. You are my magic. I absolutely love doing life with you. You are a gift from above. You are my best friend. I love you forever.

Most of all, I truly thank God for the joy of serving Him and for the opportunities He has given me over the years to share His love and His timeless message. Thank You for giving me the gift of life and the joy of doing what I love every day. It has not been a perfect journey, but You have been a perfect Shepherd, Father, and King.

FOREWORD

written by Danny's wife, Kimberly

Danny and I met our freshman year of college, and as of June 1, 2021, we've been married twenty-five years. I'm not going to lie. This milestone definitely felt like an accomplishment, a wonderful and beautiful accomplishment. We were young and naïve when we married, as many couples are, but we had a few things going for us. We had both come from divorced families and were determined to not let that happen to us. We had Christ at the center of our lives and made it our mission to keep Christ at the center of our marriage as well. Danny had already shared with me his deepest, darkest secrets (except for how he does his magic tricks), and I still wanted to be with him, because at least I knew what I was dealing with upfront.

And lastly, we had made a deal that if we ever needed help in our marriage, we would seek counseling. We may not have had more than $1,000 to our names and nowhere to live, but we were armed with those convictions. Additionally, many of the tools Danny will share with you, we learned in a weekend premarital retreat put on by Family Life called "A Weekend to Remember." We will always be grateful to the young couple who pressured us to attend and even paid for it—thank you, Cheryl and Toss.

At times, when you read Danny's words, you might think there is no way he did that or, wow, he sounds like a great guy. I can verify that all the stories are true, and yes, he is amazing and a gift from God. That being said, I don't want to be known as "the magician's wife." Yes, I'm proud of my husband for all the hard work he puts into his career as a magician, but I'm equally proud of him for being a pastor, speaker, author, husband, and the father of our three children.

And just as he wears many hats, so do I. I originally went to school to be a teacher or a counselor, but after our first child, Brian, was born, I wanted to stay home with him full-time. Twenty-one months later, the second son came along, and only two years later we started a full-time ministry of Danny traveling the world, sharing the gospel through magic. I never wanted to be on stage, so I was happy to stay home with the children and run the business side of the ministry. Trust me, it was not glamorous for either of us.

In the beginning, Danny stayed in strangers' homes on the road, while I booked events in my fun-sized closet (escaping the tiny humans I was in charge of). Not an easy time. The transition to Danny being gone on weekends but home during the week became the training ground for some of the tools Danny mentions in this book.

My least favorite question is, what does your husband do for a living? Do I say magician or pastor or author or speaker? I've decided that none of them are good options and could shut down the conversation entirely, and yet I couldn't be prouder of him. Danny is genuine, kind, passionate, full of crazy ideas, and seeks God's will every day. No, he can't make your wife disappear, and trust me, he'd never want to get rid of me. He has written this book to help you implement tricks and tips so you never want to get rid of your spouse either.

INTRODUCTION

New York. Lights. Billboards. Noise. Posters reading, "Live Tonight. Experience the death-defying underwater escape by world-renowned illusionist, Danny Ray."

I had done the escape numerous times. This time was different. The night before, while performing in Tennessee, my six-year-old daughter had watched me be shackled, submerged underwater, and locked inside a steel barrel. She was terrified and left the room almost in tears. Although this might make great theater if someone were scripting it, in real life, I couldn't stop thinking about her the following evening. My focus was completely on Caroline and not the escape.

Fifty gallons of water were dumped into a metal drum, crashing over my body, and right before the water covered my head, I said to the audience, "At some point, we're all going to take our last breath. As I go underwater, I want you to hold your breath with me, and when you let out your air, I want you to think about this: where are you going to be when you take your last breath?"

Breathing, slowing. Bringing my heart rate down.

Taking my final breath, I lowered my head under the water into a chamber that was barely large enough to hold my body. Darkness closed around me as Jeremiah, my assistant—and the only person whom I literally trusted with my life—locked me inside.

I'm usually out of the first set of handcuffs in less than a minute. Not that night. I kept thinking about the distress I had put my daughter through.

Stay focused. Focus.

Then it happened. For the first time in my eight-year professional magic career, I had made a disastrous mistake. I sucked in water. Not a lot, but enough to know I needed help immediately. The only way I could communicate with the outside world was to pull the first handcuff off and hit it against the metal chamber in pure darkness and hope that over the music Jeremiah heard me tapping to be let out. We had practiced the escape a hundred times years before, but would he remember—when it mattered?

I tried to hit my shoulder against the inside, but there wasn't enough room to make even a tiny sound.

Coughing. Spitting out water. Trying to control my breathing.

Suddenly I became aware of the darkness, and the walls of the chamber felt like they were squeezing against me.

More coughing. Spitting out water. Frantically, I tried to get the first handcuff off.

Focus.

Finally, the handcuff released, and I used the side of it against the chamber. The clink sounded so dull and muted underwater. All I could do was hope and pray that Jeremiah heard me. Then I heard him unlocking each of the six locks. He lifted the lid, and I came up coughing and gasping for air.

After what felt like forever, I caught my breath. I told Jeremiah I was fine. Time to try again, but soon I realized my focus was off again, and I needed to collect my thoughts. He got me out … again.

When I went under the third time, Jeremiah said, "This is it. Either you escape or you don't, but I'm calling it after this." I assured him I was focused, but I wasn't. That night I lost my edge. For the first time,

I didn't escape. I walked off stage in defeat. The weight of failure felt overwhelming.

After drying off, I came back onstage and humbly said, "Everybody fails. We can't give up. No matter what it takes, we must push ourselves to become the people God designed us to be. Tonight, I failed, but that's not the end. When you fail, that's only a part of your story, not the complete story. Remember that. Failure doesn't define you. God does."

Spectators came up to me after the show and made comments like "That was an amazing show!" Several people even said words to this effect: "That's the best underwater escape ever. I loved that you didn't get out so that we can wrestle with our own failures. That's so brilliant. I never would have thought how powerful a planned, failed escape attempt could be. Wow! Keep being creative."

I didn't have it in me to say, "I almost drowned. That's not what I planned."

Over the past twenty-five years of speaking, performing, pastoring, counseling, coaching, and being married to the love of my life, virtually every couple that has come to Kimberly and me for advice has struggled at times to create magic in their marriage. Maybe your marriage isn't working the way you planned, thought, or hoped it would. Maybe you feel like you're drowning or have lost focus. Maybe you're aware of all your failures and fear that your marriage will fail as well.

Whether your marriage is thriving or failing or somewhere in between, I want to give you the secrets that magicians use to create an incredible performance and show you practical ways you can implement these secrets to create an exceptional marriage by becoming a better communicator, overcoming difficulties, and celebrating life together.

Communication is the key that unlocks the door to experiencing your best marriage possible. The sooner you communicate in a loving, healthy, and respectful way, the better your marriage will be. How you deal with trials, suffering, and differences in your marriage will affect the outcome. Finally, celebrate the victories, both big and small. Be each other's best friend and have fun together. Yes, this is possible! But like any great magic trick, marriage takes practice, time, and effort.

SECTION 1

SECRETS TO COMMUNICATING EFFECTIVELY

Communication seems to be a struggle in many relationships. What I love about great communication skills is that they not only change us, but they also change our relationships forever. If you'll take the time to learn the skills presented in this section, you'll become a more effective communicator in your marriage and in your home as well as in your work and in your play.

Like magic, if you figure out how to speak to and listen to your spouse in effective ways, you obtain the one thing that matters—results. The tips and tricks in the following pages are all about helping you and your spouse hear each other and respond in a healthy, effective way. Results lead to more joy, more laughter, more fun, and more connection in your marriage.

Don't get me wrong, I'm not here to say that I have all the answers. I know that after twenty-five years of being married to the woman of my dreams, these timeless principles work.

Keep in mind, marriage is all about being a team, being on the same page. If only one of you is trying to communicate effectively and the other one isn't, that's like doing a card trick with one hand. Still possible, but limiting. If that's your situation, keep pursuing your spouse and keep loving them in intentional ways.

The secret to effective communication in marriage is simple but takes a lifetime to master. Here's the secret: speak in a loving, respectful way that your spouse can hear and that encourages them to respond to you and what you've said. If I ask Kimberly to grab a Coke for me out of the refrigerator and she brings me a jar of pickles, communication has failed—or she's sending me another message because she knows I hate pickles. Regardless, the communication didn't work, so she and I go back to the drawing board.

This section will give you the tools to develop effective communication skills that lead to results—creating magic in your marriage.

1

MISDIRECTION

Focusing on What Matters

Let your eyes look straight ahead;
fix your gaze directly before you.

—Proverbs 4:25

Misdirection is essential for creating effective illusions. Magicians know that in order to vanish a coin or make a ten-thousand-pound elephant appear, flawless misdirection is required. I love that moment in the show when audience members say to themselves, "I should've been watching that other hand!" Most people suspect that misdirection is all about having the audience look in the wrong place. In actuality, misdirection happens when the magician has the audience look in the right place at the right time. That's what creates the illusion of the impossible. That's what creates the magic.

In marriage, the goal is not an illusion of the impossible; the magic is created when we focus on the right things at the right time.

When a magician loses the ability to focus the audience's attention in the right direction, the illusion falls apart. Lose focus in your marriage and the basement couch will become your new best friend. In our marriages, it's easy to lose focus, easy to be distracted and create habits of looking in the wrong place at the wrong time.

Healthy marriages require focusing on the right things so we can have the marriage that God intended for us. What should we focus on?

Focus on Moving Toward, Not Away

Most people assume that a magician is trying to get them to look away from one object by directing them toward something else. Yes, we are directing attention away from the secret, but by pointing your attention elsewhere, we're moving our audience toward something better—a magical experience. If we directed people toward the secret, there would be no wonder and awe, no surprise, and no special moment.

In your marriage, the principle is this: move toward what will bring out the best in your marriage and away from anything that distracts and hinders that effort.

Here's an example: Let's say your spouse went out and bought a big, nonrefundable toy like a Jet Ski without checking with you or the budget. (If you're wondering what a budget is, see chapter 10). You might be upset, even furious. But guess what? You decide how you respond. Let's look at some unhealthy and healthy options.

KIMBERLY'S CORNER

Danny and I are like any other couple in that we argue and have disagreements. In the early years of our marriage, we fought about the surface-level issues. But the longer we are married, the more we realize where we need to put our focus when we disagree with each other. During the fight, we often ask ourselves these questions: What do I want out of this? How do I want this argument to end? Is this something truly important, or am I simply hungry, tired, or lonely?

Focus on communicating your needs instead of attacking your spouse. Focus on why you're feeling angry or sad. Are you hurt, disappointed, frustrated, or jealous? Focus on that emotion and communicate it.

You can react by going ballistic. You can belittle your spouse. You can use phrases like "you always" and "you never." You can take away debit and credit cards. All these reactions mean you're treating your spouse like a child instead of a partner.

Or you can show grace. You can listen. Really listen. You can try to understand your spouse's decision. You can forgive. You can press in and connect instead of pulling away and getting upset. Or better yet (since you can't return it), you can be excited about jumping on the Jet Ski and having adventures together.

Here are two strategies to help focus on moving toward each other.

1. **Create a Bonding Experience**

   Here are a few ideas to get you started.

   - Watch the sunset on your roof, a hilltop, a lake, or at the beach.
   - Picnic in the park, in your backyard, or take a drive to a favorite spot of natural beauty.
   - Make a playlist, blast your favorite tunes, and dance together.

2. **Look for Opportunities to Be Thankful**

   In 1 Thessalonians 5:17, we are reminded to "give thanks in all circumstances." Our ability to focus on being thankful positions us to be closer to our spouse. Make a game of it: how many things can I thank my spouse for?

   - Thank you for cleaning up.
   - Thank you for putting gas in my car.
   - Thank you for making the bed.
   - Thank you for choosing me today.
   - Thank you for breathing. Seriously, better breathing than not!

Focus on Loving

A friend of mine, Woody, has a septic tank on his property. About every fifteen to twenty years, he has to install a clean septic tank to get rid of everything that has ever been flushed down his toilets. This isn't a one-person job, so he invited a couple of buddies to help and started working on the project. Around noon Woody told the guys he was going to pick up lunch.

While he was gone, his two buddies decided they would pry the lid off the septic tank. As you can imagine, when they opened it, the smell was so foul and disgusting that they tried not to throw up. Then they realized one of Woody's dogs was running full speed toward the septic tank.

"No. He wouldn't," one said.

"There is no way!" said the other.

Before they could stop the dog, he leaped into the septic tank. Splash! The dog went under and didn't come up.

"Where is he? Where is he? I can't find him," they frantically shouted as they were arms deep in raw sewage trying to locate him and pull him out.

"I'm going in." The first guy jumped in. Splash! Waist-deep, he screamed, "I still can't find him! I can't find him."

Splash! The other guy jumped in.

"Got him!"

They lifted the dog out of the tank, and when his four paws hit the ground, he went crazy. He ran in circles, barking and yelping while Woody's two friends tried to chase him down. While they were running in circles covered in a hurricane of diapers, girly products, and human waste, Woody rolls up in his truck. "What the heck!"

Once the methane gas wore off the dog, the three friends spent the next several hours cleaning up the yard, the dog, and themselves. Eventually, everything was back to normal—well, as normal as can be after that kind of experience.

Sometimes marriage is a perfect storm of chaos; our relationship with our spouse feels like a hot mess. Sometimes our septic-tank story is just called Monday. But catch this: in the middle of our messes, we have a million ways to show love to our spouse. Marriage would be easy if couples could practice loving each other in perfect environments with no money problems, no family drama, and certainly no tension with each other.

But the craziness of life gives us the opportunity to laugh with our spouse and say, "Remember when we said, 'In sickness and health!' We had no idea what we were signing up for. But today in the middle of our mess, I want to remind you that I love you and there is no one else with whom I would want to navigate this storm. You are the one, baby!"

Focus on God

What you focus on changes everything. Imagine for a moment that you are holding a quarter in your hand. If you hold that quarter at arm's length, it doesn't appear that big. However, the closer you bring the quarter to your eye, the larger it appears. In fact, if you place it extremely close, the quarter can block out the entire sun. Of course, the quarter isn't larger than the sun, but it can appear larger because of how closely you are focused on it. In the same way, when you focus on the small, trivial things in your marriage, you miss out on the massive blessings and grace God has in store for you.

Daily, you decide where to focus your attention. What will you choose? If you focus on lack of money, that struggle will appear disproportionately large. If you focus on God who provides for birds of the air, the fish of the sea, and the flowers in the field, then you'll be reminded of God's power, His miraculous provision, His constant care for His people, and you'll be reminded that He will sustain you.

Focusing on God looks different for each couple, but here are some tips and tricks to try.

1. **Debrief Together**
   If you attend church together, find ways of implementing the weekly messages you hear into your everyday life. Knowing that you're going to talk about the message helps you to stay focused and actively engaged in listening.
2. **Read a Great Book or Listen to a Podcast Together**
   There are lots of great books and podcast to choose from. Find one that will challenge both of you to grow in your faith.
3. **Serve Together**
   Serving others together helps a couple grow in their faith and gain perspective. This kind of shared experience can have a profound impact on your relationship.
4. **Play Together**
   Find an activity or two that you enjoy doing together and talk about what God has been teaching you while you walk, ride bikes, or kayak as a couple.

The principle of misdirection is all about focusing on the right things at the right time. In marriage, it's easy to get offtrack, distracted, or caught up in our jobs, our kids, our activities, and to forget to invest in our spouse. The tips and tricks from this chapter will help you focus like a magician and create magic in your marriage.

CREATING MAGIC TOGETHER

TAKEAWAY

Focus is important in marriage. If we don't focus on right thoughts and actions, our focus can wander and bring bad habits and unwanted patterns into our marriages.

QUESTIONS

Go to your favorite restaurant and leave your phones in your car. Ask these questions:

1. What is something I can focus on this week that would be helpful to you?
2. What things are distracting us from communicating better?

PLAN OF ACTION

Share one way that each of you are going to focus on communicating more effectively. Look back through the chapter for ideas.

SECRETS KILL

Magicians Have Secrets, Marriages Don't

> *Therefore confess your sins to each other and pray for each other so that you may be healed. The prayer of a righteous person is powerful and effective.*
>
> —James 5:16

Secrets are for magicians, not marriages. As a magician, I don't keep secrets from people; I keep secrets for people. If I shared the secrets of my illusions, the audience would miss out on the wonder, the magic, and the astonishment of a great show.

In a marriage, secrets destroy trust, kill hope, and cause spouses to miss out on the beautiful friendship they could have with each other. Secrets in marriage never bring out the wonder, magic, and astonishment of a great relationship.

Kimberly and I graduated from college one Saturday in 1996, married the following Saturday, lived in a friend's laundry room for two weeks, and then moved to Colorado. That was the start of our new adventure together. The first year was quite a ride!

I was in seminary working on my Master of Divinity degree at the time, so I put in lots of late nights and early mornings. Kimberly and I both worked long hours as we navigated this thing called marriage.

We had plenty of normal ups and downs, but one moment in particular arose when I had to decide what kind of husband I was going to be for my wife.

She was at work, and I was driving home when I saw a neon sign for a shop that simply read Magazines. The trappings of pornography were a part of my old life and old struggles before I became a believer. Even early on, Kimberly and I had a great sex life, so I was good, right? But like a drug addict, I was drawn toward those lights. My heart pounded when I entered that seedy, dark store. Nude posters covered the walls, and dirty magazines lined the shelves throughout the shop. I stayed for a minute, then left in shame.

After I got back in my car, a million thoughts went through my mind: What am I doing? This isn't who I am anymore. Why? I'm married now. I shouldn't desire that stuff. Kimberly is beautiful and amazing. Why aren't I satisfied by her alone? Why do I want more? What's going on?

In the Garden of Eden, God gave Adam and Eve a simple test of trust: Would they follow God's instruction or listen to someone else? They chose to reject God, and instead of telling Him the truth, the first thing they did after their disobedience was go into hiding. Humanity has been responding the same way ever since.

In the parking lot of the porn store, I faced a similar decision: was I going to start our marriage in hiding or tell my wife the truth?

I wrestled with this decision over and over. I justified that going into the store wasn't a big deal. After all, I didn't do anything. I didn't stay that long. I didn't buy anything. Yet my lustful desires were there, and I didn't know why, so I decided not to hide, not to keep secrets from my wife. Full of shame and embarrassment, I told her.

We ended up in counseling together for several months. But the act of confession, the choice to not hide from Kimberly and to receive professional help started us down a road to healing and a lifetime of bringing our failures to each other.

James 5:16 instructs us to "confess your sins to each another and pray for each another so that you may be healed." Confessing to your spouse can be deeply painful. You might feel like you're letting them down and disappointing them. But in the confession, you build trust. Without confession there can be no healing of the relationship or the soul. And sometimes when one person confesses, the other person feels free to also confess their mistakes, sins, and mess-ups as well.

The verse in James doesn't stop with confession; it also includes "pray for each another." In combination, prayer and confession lead to healing. Obedience to this verse can stop the unfortunate cycle many couples are caught in: They go to God and confess their sins. They repent and tell God, "I will never do this or that again." And they don't—but then they do. So, they go back to God and promise fervently, "I will never do it again!" Then they do and the cycle continues.

Confessing to "each other" breaks the secret life that brings division, while praying for each other brings the healing power of God that leads to restoration and unity.

Maybe you're saying to yourself, "But you don't know what I've done. I've kept secrets for years." If that's you, answer these questions: Would you rather live a lie, protect your secret, and continue a superficial relationship with your spouse? Or would you rather take the risk of sharing the truth and seek to be forgiven, to be shown grace, and to be loved as you are? Sharing the truth can lead to peace and healing, a fulfilling life, and a fantastic marriage. Lies cause an enormous amount of stress, create weak relationships, and fracture trust. Always choose truth.

Unpacking the past, especially past secrets, can be scary. I'm not suggesting that you bring up everything from your past and dump it all on your spouse at once, because that could cause a different kind of tension. However, secrets hinder our marriages and can't be ignored. Maybe you need to reach out to a counselor or bring in a trusted third party to start unpacking secrets that hinder intimacy in your marriage.

The point is, sharing should lead toward healing and freedom, and those two qualities help create a healthier marriage.

If you or your spouse has secrets to share, here are four essentials to experiencing healing and reconciliation through sharing.

1. Safe to Share

Before you share everything freely, which I encourage you to do, create a safe place to share. There are too many variables in creating a safe sharing place to simply say, "Do it this way." For example, if your spouse is belligerent when drunk, that's a bad time to share something private or personal. You can't control how your spouse will respond to your confession, but you can attempt to create the best possible environment for success.

Patterns you've previously established when one of you blows it will also factor into setting up the right space. Ideally, you want to provide uninterrupted time to share and to allow a response. This might mean you need to hire a babysitter. This might mean you need to take time off work. The key is that you create a designated time and location where you and your spouse can sit down, look into each other's eyes, and confess your struggles or issues.

Creating a safe place to share ultimately builds trust in your relationship. As you build trust, there will be opportunities to share frequently, in almost any location.

2. Courage to Share

When I'm performing, timing affects the reactions of the crowd. If I say, "Look, your coin has vanished," but the audience still sees it in my hand, and then three seconds later, it vanishes, I've created confusion. Believe me, confusion is not magic. When they see the coin after I tell them that it vanished, they don't know if something went wrong or if I am joking. However, if I show a coin in my hand, and it disappears the instant I snap my fingers, the crowd feels like something magical happened. When it comes to sharing something important with your spouse, timing is everything.

So, before you rush into sharing something that could be devastating, painful, or difficult to take in, soak in Psalm 27:14: "Wait for the LORD; be strong and take heart and wait for the Lord." Wait for God's timing. Listen to His voice. Be strong. Listen to wise counsel. After waiting, listening, and preparing, have the courage to share.

3. Understanding Your Spouse's Needs

To fool an audience with a spectacular magic trick, thousands of little things have to happen: find the right trick, practice it, figure out the right presentation (the words I say), and prepare the necessary props. Then when I perform the trick, the audience needs to be engaged, the lighting needs to be right, the crowd needs to be able to see the magic clearly, and I need to maintain a good connection with the audience. The timing, the sleight of hand, and the misdirection need to be flawless. I can go on and on, but everything needs to be in its proper place for the audience to react with astonishment.

You see, the relationship between a magician and the audience is symbiotic. If my goal is to astonish the audience, then I can't do whatever I want. As a magician, I need to think about what is best for the audience and how I can create the best experience for them. The best effects happen when I think about the audience first.

In the same way, our best marriage occurs when we put our spouse first. And like a good trick, thousands of little things need to be in place for a marriage to thrive instead of survive.

Sometimes, in our marriages, we assume that our spouse's needs are the same as our own. When you come home, you might need five minutes to unwind while your spouse needs an hour. You might desire sex five nights a week, but your spouse is satisfied with twice a month.

You might enjoy going for an hour-long run, but your spouse might enjoy being on the couch for two hours. These differences are good, and they are part of the way God has wired you. The goal isn't to make your spouse be exactly like you or to force them to enjoy exactly what you enjoy. Instead, the goal is to understand your spouse and to help them become exactly who God designed them to be.

A game-changing tool for our marriage came from *The Five Love Languages*. In that book, Dr. Gary Chapman talks about each of us having a primary way that we experience love. My wife's primary love language is acts of slavery—I mean, service. So, when I vacuum the house, it is pretty much like foreplay to her. (The other four love languages are words of affirmation, physical touch, receiving gifts, and quality time.)

Over the years, my primary love language has changed a little, but my top ones are physical touch and quality time. Knowing Kimberly's love language has helped me to love her and serve her in a way that she can truly feel it, and she has grown to understand my love language in a way that communicates clearly with me.

Early on in our marriage when we were ready to resolve an argument, I gave her a hug (remember, my love language is physical touch), and she would tell me, "I'm sorry" (her love language is acts of service, and humble confession is an act of service). Yet at the end of resolving the argument, we both still felt hurt and had a difficult time moving forward because we didn't know what the other person needed for closure. We both wrongly thought that the other person needed exactly what we needed.

If I had told her "I'm sorry," she would have felt better, and if she had given me a hug, I would have felt better because we would have been meeting each other's felt needs. *The Five Love Languages* helped us realize that we needed to respond to each other in a way that matched our love language. Over time, we learned to resolve arguments by meeting the other person's needs instead of our own. Like a good magician, we had to put the audience first.

A simple question you can ask each other is, what helps you move on after an argument? Or check out Kimberly's thoughts on using the language of what can I do to make you feel better?

4. Accountability

I've traveled for almost two decades, performing over four thousand shows in all fifty states and in twenty-one countries. During these years, I've been hit on by a few women, been put into hotels next to strip clubs, and experienced a variety of scenarios that could have compromised my relationship with Kimberly. However, one habit changed our ministry from the beginning because of some expert advice given by

KIMBERLY'S CORNER

It always bothered me when little children on the playground went to the teacher to tattle on one another, and the teacher said, "Say sorry. Now go play." I even prayed about this issue when I was teaching preschool in Colorado many years ago. The Bible teaches us how to reconcile with one another, and that reconciliation is vital in our relationships.

I had no problem teaching this principle to our children, so when they hurt each other, it was never enough to say, "Sorry." They needed to apologize and then ask what they could do to make the other person feel better. Sometimes, the children responded by saying they wanted a hug, or they responded with "please don't do that again."

A little more difficult for me, but still essential, is to ask Danny what I can do to make him feel better after I have hurt him (he does the same for me). It is humbling, I admit, but finding out how you can make the other person feel better is the reconciliation component. So try it. The next time you get into an argument or do something (even accidentally) that may have hurt your spouse, ask them what you can do to make them feel better. Trust me, it's freeing and beautiful.

author and comedian, Ken Davis. He told me, "Danny, as soon as you can afford it, have someone travel with you. It's a game changer." From day one, someone has traveled with me to keep me accountable (and to run live video).

Staying focused on the road is so much easier when I can share my struggles with someone and ask him to keep me on track. Bringing someone else on the road created shared experiences, helped me build great friendships, and kept me focused as it helped keep my marriage strong. On a regular basis, I watch people compromise their values on the road because no one is holding them accountable for their actions. If you find yourself traveling for work, I highly recommend you have someone travel with you or keep you accountable on the road. It's hard out there. On the financial end, a travel companion never makes sense. It always cost more money to have someone travel with me, but I would rather lose profit than integrity.

In the rare situation when I am on my own on the road, I talk to my accountability partners and tell them my plan of action to stay pure. Usually, I start with a simple phone call. I tell them where I'm going, what I'm doing, and what times I'll be by myself. I ask them to keep me in their prayers and to call me at certain times when temptations might be higher.

I've also memorized 2 Timothy 2:22 and other verses that remind me to not just run from temptation but also to run toward something good. Remembering that the rewards of living for God are so much better than the chains of the old life has been a great weapon in my own journey of accountability.

Learning to be vulnerable and share secrets leads to healing and a better relationship, while unleashing the power of God's grace and forgiveness in your marriage. Secrets kill hope, kill trust, and ultimately kill the relationship.

Secrets are great for magicians, not for marriages!

CREATING MAGIC TOGETHER

TAKEAWAY

Try implementing this simple concept every month. Go out for a secret drink date. Buy your favorite coffee, juice, or cocktail and once your drink arrives, it's time for the second part of the date. Share a secret! The only rule is that it's something your spouse doesn't know. You can share a silly secret from childhood, a wild secret from youth, a funny or embarrassing secret that happened recently, or something that needs to come out in your relationship.

QUESTIONS

What's a secret you have been keeping? How long have you kept that secret? Would it be hurtful to someone, especially your spouse, if you revealed it? Share that with your spouse and start fresh in that secret area.

PLAN OF ACTION

Rejoice together that you have shared a secret with each other. Celebrate that the secret is no longer one-sided but shared. From this point forward, vow never to keep secrets from your mate.

3

HOW TO READ MINDS

Understanding How Your Spouse Thinks

Be kind to one another, tenderhearted, forgiving one another, as God in Christ forgave you.

—Ephesians 4:32 ESV

The best mind readers who study body language, have an uncanny ability to observe the smallest details, gather information surreptitiously, ask the right questions, and listen to everything. An old joke among mentalists (those who supposedly read minds) goes like this: you know it's bad when you have to put your glasses on to read someone's mind.

Most of what a mind reader practices happens in a few seconds. Imagine you're at an intimate theater that seats seventy guests. You feel the excitement and the thrill as you wait for the curtain to open, knowing you're about to experience mind reading firsthand.

Before the show started, the performer heard someone talking about losing their dad a year ago on this date. As the curtain lifts, he performs a few initial mind-reading stunts, then he brings up Elizabeth (the one who lost her dad). When he greets her onstage, he notices smoke stains on her fingers. He files this information, wondering if she might be compulsive or anxious, and he assumes she has other addictions. Her smile is bright from teeth whitening, which might indicate she's trying to hide something. From her firm handshake and direct eye contact, he gathers that she has a high-profile job.

The mind reader says, "Please sit. Have we ever met?" You are riveted by his showmanship, confidence, and immediate connection with her.

Elizabeth shakes her head. "Never."

He says, "I'd like to try something. Please just nod if I'm correct. This doesn't always work, but I'm going to try to unlock something that is only within your mind."

Elizabeth agrees.

He moves on. "You have great confidence in who you are, but recently that has been shaken. You've been more anxious than usual (she nods). You've been trying to cover up, yet you stand tall and strong. But today is different (she is trying not to cry). Today is significant because this date matters to you more than most. Today you're reminded of your origins (a tear slips out) and of who you are meant to be. Today is a reminder to love those who surround you because time is short."

The audience gasps at the accuracy of the mind reader. It's unbelievable how he apparently knew so much in so little time.

Information Is the Key

If you're going to learn to read your spouse's mind, take some lessons from a mind reader. To read minds, you need information. In the scenario above, the mind reader spent less than a minute with Elizabeth and never asked one question related to her past. Imagine what he could do if he asked questions. The more information a mind reader has, the more detailed and amazing his mind reading will be. Information is the key.

Unlike the mind reader, you and I aren't trying to entertain an audience; we're trying to love our spouses the way God intended. We have the freedom to gather a lot of information over time and observe their habits, patterns, and behaviors so we can learn to respond to them in the best possible way.

A good mentalist studies everything about how people think and respond to the world around them; he then uses this information to create the illusion of mind reading. We can learn to study our spouse's behavior, patterns, personality, and preferences and use our knowledge to love them, encourage them, care for them, and build them up.

Our job is to use the information to help them. In 1 Thessalonians 5:11, Paul tells us, "Therefore encourage one another and build each other up, just as in fact you are doing." These two practices, encouragement and building each other up, change the outcome of any conversation.

Husbands, imagine that your wife comes home from work, flops on the couch, and says, "I'm so exhausted." You now have a lot of information. You know she had a long, rough day at work. She told you she is mentally exhausted, and she is physically tired (she flopped on the couch).

Here's what you shouldn't say:

"Hey babe, what's for dinner tonight?" Let me

KIMBERLY'S CORNER

No matter who you are, you want to feel heard and understood by the important people in your life. Here's an amazing trick: when your husband or wife is talking, stop thinking about what you're going to say next.

When we listen with the intent to respond, we miss things. But when we listen well, we can hear the other person's tone and maybe the heart or motive behind what is shared with us.

Try listening and summarizing what you heard. You can even say, "I think what you're saying is that you hate when I leave my clothes all over the floor because it makes you feel like I don't care about you or our home. Is that right?" After you summarize, ask your spouse to confirm you understand correctly.

read her mind for you. She isn't making dinner! In fact, she's ordering pizza and may not be ordering enough for you.

Or

"Glad you're here. The kids need help with their homework. I'm heading out with the guys." Good luck explaining your black eye to the boys!

Or

"Don't forget, tonight the kids are out. It's our night to 'get it on,' right?" Prepare for a night of disappointment!

Instead, use the information she gave you to encourage and build her up. There isn't one right way to respond to this situation, but here are a few ways that could be helpful in loving her and supporting her.

1. Ask Questions

Sometimes, even mind readers can make mistakes or misread the information they have gathered. The key to being right is to collect more information so you can be more accurate. Questions are the key to getting information, and information is the key to mind reading.

You might ask questions such as these: Which coworker do I need to make disappear permanently? Seems like you had a rough day. Do you want to talk about it? A year from now, what do you think will be funny about this day? Was the entire day terrible? Questions are a way to continue the conversation, and they give you the opportunity to gather more information.

2. Listen

When she says, "I'm exhausted!" you could say, "Tell me about it," and then listen. Don't try to fix the problem. Don't make excuses for her coworkers. Don't give her solutions on how she could handle herself better next time. Nope. Only listen.

Listening can encourage her because sometimes we feel like nobody is listening to us. So, turn off your phone or any other distractions and listen, trying to understand why she's exhausted. Remember James 1:19 tells us, "Everyone should be quick to listen, slow to speak and slow to become angry." Jumping to conclusions is easy, but it is always better, initially, to just listen.

If you think of information or advice that may help your spouse, don't tell her. Timing is everything. She might not be ready to hear you at that moment. Instead ask, "Is now a good time to share something that I think might be helpful, or would you rather I save it for later?" That kind of response lets your wife know that you heard her, that you care, and that she can decide whether she wants your input now or later.

3. Clarify

Without question, clarity is the secret sauce to mind reading. After you've gathered information, use it to clarify, precisely, your spouse's present needs. In the past, when your wife has been exhausted, what did she need? Let's say every time she's exhausted, she wants to wind down by watching her favorite show. Ask her, "Do you want to share anything else? No? Okay, would you like me to put on your favorite TV show?" She may tell you that would be fantastic, or she may tell you something else. The key is to clarify what she needs and help her meet those needs.

4. Take Action

If, while you were listening, she says, "I really want to eat ice cream and relax in a bath." Guess what! It will seem like you are reading her mind if, after she watches her show, you say, "Why don't I get the bath going and bring you some ice cream?"

You listened and clarified what you heard. You knew exactly what she wanted because she told you. Like the audience watching the mentalist, your wife will marvel, thinking, how did he know I wanted that? You, my friend, have become a mind reader.

5. Remember Expectations

Part of what makes the mentalist's work easy is that the audience is expecting him or her to dazzle them with their skill. Every little observed detail adds to the expectation and leaves the audience with greater awe. In the same way, knowing your spouse's expectations helps avoid unnecessary tension between the two of you and positions you to serve her real needs, not her perceived needs. For the last twenty-five years, Kimberly and I have made it a pattern to know each other's expectations when either of us comes home from work.

Imagine you call your wife on her way home from work and ask, "How was your day?" Then you listen when she tells you she is exhausted and had a rough day. After you clarify what she needs, you spring into action. When she arrives home to her favorite TV show (ding, we've got a winner!) on a laptop (check yes!) with a bowl of ice cream sitting next to the bathtub (with just enough bubbles to soothe away an awful day), you will win Husband of the Year. Congratulations, you are a mind reader.

Now, ladies, do you want to know the secret to reading his mind? Simply show up naked. The end.

All joking aside (mostly), the principles are the same for men. The outcome and the needs are different from person to person, but you still need to ask, listen, clarify, and then take action while remembering expectations. In doing so, your spouse will think you are a marriage mentalist. Sure, men may leak information out rather than pour it out, but a good marriage mentalist can sift through that data and amaze their spouse.

Mind reading isn't a perfect science. You have needs and desires too, and that's where things can become messy. Yet, if you're both looking to read each other's minds, you will find opportunities to encourage and build each other up.

Mind Reading Made Simple

Mind reading is a skill that involves gathering the information, asking the right questions, and clarifying your spouse's needs and desires. In doing this, you'll learn to know your spouse better and better, and you'll be able to read their mind like a pro.

CREATING MAGIC TOGETHER

TAKEAWAY

Listening is an important part of every relationship for many reasons. In a marriage, you can learn your spouse's likes and dislikes and discover new ways to surprise him or her with acts of love and kindness.

QUESTIONS

Can you help me understand how you think? Would you be willing to explain your thinking more completely when I'm acting confused or clueless?

1. What can I do this week to help you? (Please tell me because I'm terrible at guessing.)

PLAN OF ACTION

Develop a plan for helping each other become a better mind reader. If there is an important hint you're trying to give your mate, develop a signal that will encourage your mate to listen carefully. Say, "Ding, ding, ding!" or tap him or her on the hand in a certain way as a reminder.

4

SCRIPTING

What You Say, When You Say It, and How You Say It Matters

> *It is better to keep your mouth closed and let people think you are a fool than to open it and remove all doubt.*
>
> —Mark Twain[1]

Everything a magician says is integral to creating a perfect illusion. The script (everything the performer says and does) is crafted to create clarity, precise timing, and perfect tempo. Without these elements, the show falls apart.

Clarity: If what the magician does isn't clear, the illusion fails.

Timing: If what the magician says is said at the wrong time, the illusion fails.

Tempo: If what the magician means is lost because of the speed at which it's performed, the illusion fails.

Like creating magic, great communication requires clarity, timing, and tempo. When we are clear in our communication, speak at the right time, and monitor the tempo of the conversation, we'll position ourselves to thrive in our relationship. Let's look at how these skills can take our communication to the next level.

Scripting

Whether or not you're aware of it, we all have scripts in our marriages. Have you and your spouse ever had the same fight you had before? It's almost as if the two of you have a script. Even though you hate that this fight happens again, you know your part and play your role. The longer you're married, the more you'll have to work on breaking unhealthy scripts. If we're aware of both the healthy and unhealthy scripts, we can improve our communication skills and prevent the crazy cycle.

KIMBERLY'S CORNER

Not only does what you say matter but also to whom you say it. Another way we can honor and show respect to our spouse is by keeping the negative stuff private. In other words, if you have a fight or don't like something your spouse did, don't talk to your coworkers, parents, or children about it. And definitely don't talk to another man about your husband—or another woman about your wife. You are asking for trouble!

When you share about someone else's faults, they aren't able to share their side of what happened. You only convey how you experienced the event, which isn't fair to the other person. Additionally, if you share with your mother how hurt you were when your spouse came home late and forgot your anniversary, your mother will most likely feel hurt with you and for you. That might make you feel better at the time, but the problem is that your mother (in this example) will often hold a bit of a grudge. You may have worked through the disagreement and forgiven your spouse, but your mother has not had a chance to reconcile and forgive the offense, and it's not okay for her to address it because it has nothing to do with her.

So, if you need to vent about something that happened, call a therapist, not your mother.

To experience the happiness God has in store for your marriage, you'll need to discard some old scripts and replace them with scripts that bring *clarity* to the situation, are *timed* to meet each other's needs, and are more focused on the *tempo* of the whole conversation than on fast-forwarding to winning an argument.

Clarity

Clarity empowers us to be effective communicators. As an entertainer, it's essential that I'm clear about what I have to offer. If people come to my show and I start to do ventriloquism, they'll be shocked and disappointed. (Not only were they hoping to see magic, but I'm a terrible ventriloquist!) If I tell them I'm going to make an elephant disappear, and instead I vanish a car, they'll be impressed by the car, but they'll be confused and ask themselves, "What about the elephant?"

If you tell your spouse one thing and then do another, you not only create confusion. but you also miss an opportunity to build trust. And trust is fundamental to creating a healthy marriage. In a performance, clarity builds trust with my audience. In a marriage, clarity builds trust with your spouse.

Let's say your husband notices you have a grocery list for a birthday party you're planning. He says, "Would it help if I went to the grocery store?" You are so thankful he noticed, and you would love the extra help. However, getting the groceries in your mind means buying your normal groceries as well as the extra stuff on the birthday list.

So, when he comes home with only the items on the birthday list, you're disappointed. He feels great because he noticed the list, you didn't have to ask him, and he went shopping to help you out. The lack of clarity about what it means to grocery shop has a high chance of leading to an argument.

Your husband is genuinely looking for an opportunity to help, which is great. The key is to clearly define what you mean by grocery list. This might seem trivial, because to you it's obvious that since you're at the store, you should pick up everything you need, not just the few items required for the birthday party. From his side, he can probably think of times where you wanted him to rush to the grocery store to get one item for which you had an immediate need. It can be confusing—so the key to communicating more effectively is to say specifically what you want and expect.

Clarity changes the outcome of every conversation. To avoid unhealthy frustration, ask questions like "So we are clear, are you saying ..." or "I'm not sure what you mean, could you help me understand?" When your expectations are clear, your spouse will be able to meet those expectations and create the best outcome possible.

Timing

Recently, I returned home from a long trip, and Kimberly was overwhelmed by the status of the house. The next day, while she was out, I decided to clean the house for her. I started with the kitchen and made my way into the living room, where I noticed dust on some of the furniture. I was going to grab a cloth to wipe things down, but I wanted to do a superb job.

That's when a wonderful idea came into my head—I should use a leaf blower. Yes, that's what I needed to clean all the dust! Now, I don't know if you have ever turned on a 75-mph leaf blower in your house, but it's, well—amazing!

I'm not sure why, but the first place I pointed my new dust buster was under the stove. Not only did I blow dust out, but a Pokemon card and a swirl of other toys also evacuated their shelter.

Before I knew it, I was pointing this thing under the fridge and on top of the china cabinet. I wouldn't have been surprised had a tumbleweed blown by as huge clouds of dust engulfed me.

For a moment I felt like the king of my castle! I dusted everything imaginable, and after ten minutes of work, I turned the blower off to survey the landscape. While I had successfully dusted, it also looked like a hurricane had swept through our house.

Imagine what happened when I heard my wife's car pull into the driveway. *Do I greet her at the front door holding my leaf blower?* How does one explain a great idea gone wrong? Let's just say, timing is everything.

If your husband dropped dinner on the floor and is yelling at the mashed potatoes, it might be the wrong time to tell him he has an anger problem.

If your wife is driving too fast and there is a cop behind her, it might be the wrong time to point out that she wouldn't need to drive so fast if she woke up earlier and didn't jumpstart her day with fifteen cups of coffee.

What you say, when you say it, and how you say it matters.

Poor timing in our communication often leads to defensiveness. Shifting blame is common when we're hurt, covering up a mistake, or falling into an old script. Instead, deal with the current situation and try to avoid piling on with old content. Own your part and take responsibility. Apologize when appropriate, and work on forgiveness and reconciliation. Then, at the right time (another time), you can address what your spouse is or isn't doing.

Making a small change in timing will make a big difference in creating healthy communication.

Tempo

A great song requires the right tempo. Some parts are slow, some fast, and if it all works together, you can create beautiful music. Communication requires tempo too. Tempo, in arguments, is about being fast to forgive, slow to anger, quick to be patient, and thoughtful in what you say.

One of the most valuable phrases Kimberly and I use to change the tempo of a conversation is "this is important to me." We only use that phrase a few times a year. If we're having a heated discussion and she doesn't feel like I recognize its importance to her, she says, "This is important to me." Those words stop me in my tracks, and because we use them infrequently, they've become a game changer in our conversations.

When we use the phrase properly, the other person instantly becomes aware that something is going on beneath the surface conversation. A wound is being poked. This phrase gives us the ability to change the tempo in the heat of the conversation and helps us avoid saying things we'll regret.

Tempo matters. James 1:19 says, "Everyone should be quick to listen, slow to speak and slow to become angry." The rhythm with which you speak and listen directly impacts the outcome of a conversation with your spouse.

If you struggle to be slow to anger and quick in grace, you don't only have a tempo problem, you have a heart problem. Thankfully, God is slow to anger. He is also merciful, gracious, and the healer of the heart. Let's unpack the words of Jesus: "For the mouth speaks what the heart is full of" (Luke 6:45).

The words we speak to our spouse are a direct reflection of what's in our heart. This is an unavoidable truth. We can blame our spouse for setting us off or pushing our buttons, but if we're spewing venom out of our mouth, the reality is that our heart is overflowing with that poison. Look at Jesus' words again: what we say and how we say it are a direct result of what's going on inside of us.

If I fill a glass with water, that's what comes out when I empty it. If I fill the glass with prune juice, prune juice comes out. If I fill it with cow dung, cow dung comes out. This is simple science.

In the same way, if we speak in a harmful, derogatory, and disrespectful way, our heart needs help, not our spouse's. All the practical tips in the world are useless to us if we don't deal with the root problem—God needs to heal our heart.

To change what's coming out of your mouth, change what's going into your heart. This process takes time, but the beauty about heart problems is that God says He will "give you a new heart and put a new spirit in you; I will remove from you your heart of stone and give you a heart of flesh" (Ezekiel 36:26).

God is in the business of removing old, bitter, and hateful hearts, and replacing them with brand-new ones that beat for Him. This is why God pursues us with His love daily. This is why God sent Jesus to die in our place. This is why the resurrection of Jesus from the dead matters for our marriages. God loves us so much that even though we don't deserve it, He gives us a new heart and a new life. In this new life we become His child, and our new heart enables us to love our spouse with the sacrificial love with which He loves us; it also equips us to pursue our spouse the way God constantly pursues us. We can live out of the newness of God's gift, not out of our old, broken life.

Scripting

To experience fresh ways of communicating, we need to rewrite our scripts to include clarity, timing, and tempo. We can't hide behind old excuses, past wounds, hidden agendas, or harmful habits. We need God's Spirit to flow through our lives, exposing those hidden patterns of communication that have failed and revealing the unhealthy communication that weighs us down.

Writing new scripts is hard work, and your heart might be scarred by years of poor communication and neglect. But the risk is worth the effort.

Decide how you can change the clarity, timing, and tempo of the scripts in your marriage. Think about one fight you and your spouse have had over and over again. Now, think about new words you can use to resolve the issue, a new location to talk about it, and a new heart that chooses to listen instead of yielding to anger. This process will help you change the script, and discarding unhealthy scripts will bring new life to the marriage.

Let's take an imaginary script and see if we can use the techniques above to turn it around.

Walking in the door, you're greeted with these words: "Hey baby, I talked to my parents, and they're coming over for dinner. I can't wait. It's been forever."

"We just saw them last week."

"You always say that. It was eight ... e-i-g-h-t days ago, idiot."

"Whatever! Same thing."

"Can you just get the BBQ going? They're on their way."

"Why? So your dad can critique my homemade sauce?"

"You know his is better."

"Yeah, and you look just like your mom."

Okay, this conversation is a train wreck. Name-calling. Assumptions. Blaming. Comparison. Poor timing.

Now, let's create a new script.

Before calling your parents, you talk to your husband and obtain *clarity* that he is okay with them coming over, and he is good to barbecue. You tell him how you love his BBQ sauce. You have that conversation with your husband after finding out the best *time* to talk to him. Then you discuss the best *tempo* (tonight, tomorrow, when hell freezes over) for making the night a reality. Can you see how different the conversation might be when clarity, timing, and tempo are considered?

Replacing unhealthy scripts with better ones will create magic in your marriage. This might feel like a massive change to make, so start with one script and see if you can generate a little magic one changed script at a time.

CREATING MAGIC TOGETHER

TAKEAWAY

Good communication is a matter of clarity, timing, and tempo. What you say, when you say it, and how you say it matters. You may not mean to sound curt, demanding, or controlling, but sometimes you don't pay attention to how your words may sound to your mate. Thinking about a recent argument, how could you change your words, tone, or timing to create a different outcome?

QUESTIONS

1. What's one script we need to change?
2. How can we change this script using clarity, timing, and tempo? (Remember, it's not about winning.)

PLAN OF ACTION

Have a conversation using the new script. Give grace and start again if necessary.

5

DEALING WITH HECKLERS

Resolving Conflict

> *Do not let any unwholesome talk come out of your mouths, but only what is helpful for building others up according to their needs, that it may benefit those who listen.*
>
> —Ephesians 4:29

Heck·ler /ˈhek(ə)lər/: a person who interrupts a performer or public speaker with derisive or aggressive comments or abuse.

For centuries, performers have dealt with hecklers. Early 1900s vaudeville theater incorporated hecklers into plays, and regular hecklers were a significant part of popular TV programs and variety shows, including Statler and Waldorf on *The Muppet Show*.

When I was fifteen, I worked at a San Diego restaurant called The Gathering. My job was to go from table to table, doing magic for the patrons. Over the years, this led to performing at cocktail parties and banquets, where I encountered my first heckler. I was performing for a small group at a company banquet when a guy grabbed the deck out of my hands and exclaimed, "I know how you did that. Watch!" He caught me so off guard that I wasn't sure what to do when he revealed the secret of my trick to everyone in the group.

What he didn't know was that even at sixteen, I knew ten other ways to do the same trick. He only knew one. I took the knowledge he had and used it against him. While the deck was still in his hands, I said, "Reach in and grab out one card, any card. Don't look at it."

He immediately covered it with his hands and said in a condescending voice, "Go ahead, name this card, hot shot." Keep in mind, this is a grown man, and I was a sixteen-year-old kid.

Of course, I named his card. He freaked out, and in a matter of moments, he was fooled again. He became my biggest fan, telling people, "You've gotta see this guy. I thought I knew how it was done, but he showed me!"

That day forever changed the way I view conflict. I've seen countless performers lose control of their audience because they go head-to-head with a heckler. But the key to working with hecklers is to get them on your side. That's why those early TV shows incorporated hecklers—audiences loved it.

The same is true when it comes to conflict in your marriage. Marriage isn't a contest between you and your spouse. You both need to be on the same side, the same team.

What if you could see conflict through a different lens? Sometimes people see conflict as something to avoid in a relationship instead of something neutral that can strengthen their marriage. First Corinthians 10:31 says, "So whether you eat or drink or whatever you do, do it all for the glory of God." Notice the verse says, "whatever you do." We are called to bring glory to God in whatever we do and that includes what we say and do in a heated argument.

Depending on your personality, you might prefer to run away from conflict so you don't have to deal with the issue. Or maybe you enjoy a good fight, and you see an argument as your chance to win, to prove you're right. But neither of those responses brings glory to God. One avoids issues so that problems build up over time. The other response forgets that marriage is a team sport. If one spouse wins and the other loses, you both lose. The better approach is to engage each other with the goal of being on the same team—Team Us.

This might seem too lofty. After all, you've had the same fights for years, you've prayed about it, and maybe you think you've tried everything. But what if you could work through the tension, the conflict, the anger, and the fight? What if on the other side there was hope, grace, joy, and life for your marriage? Wouldn't it be worth the pain to resolve the conflict, if you could move toward each other and end up loving each other even more?

Tips and Tricks to Resolving Conflict

As a magician, I constantly try to solve problems in different ways. As a pastor, I look for ways to help people experience the fullness of life. In other words, my job is to give people a fresh perspective on living life to the fullest. To create the best marriage possible, we need a new way of looking at conflict.

Consider a deck of cards. Once it has been shuffled several times, there is almost no chance you will ever see it in that same order again. In fact, it would be more likely for you to win the lottery every day for the rest of your life than for you to see a deck shuffled in the same order twice. That's not hyperbole—it's math! The combinations of fifty-two cards are fifty-two factorials, which means that the probability of having any shuffled deck in the same order as another shuffled deck is astronomical.

Despite this fact, I know numerous ways to bring order to the chaos of a shuffled deck. If you hand me a shuffled deck, I can create the illusion that I control every card in the deck. In a matter of minutes, I can restore the deck to perfect order. This is possible because, although there are a gazillion combinations for shuffling a deck, there is only one way to restore the deck to brand-new order. The same is true in marriage. Although there might be a billion ways to get into an argument, there is only one way to make it right.

So how do you make it right? God's way. I feel like that is cheating (almost a cop-out to say "God's way"), but I want to look at how we can resolve our conflicts in a healthy, godly way.

> James 4:1–3 explains why we have many of our fights:
>
> What causes fights and quarrels among you? Don't they come from your desires that battle within you? You desire but do not have, so you kill. You covet but you cannot get what you want, so you quarrel and fight. You do not have because you do not ask God. When you ask, you do not receive, because you ask with wrong motives, that you may spend what you get on your pleasures.

Think about what this passage says. Your arguments come from unmet desires. You want something and you don't receive it, so you fight. Kimberly and I say that every one of our arguments can be traced back to someone's unmet expectations. Think about the last couple of arguments you and your spouse had. What was at the root of the conflict? Probably an unmet expectation. The cool part is that this means we can prevent a ton of arguments by clarifying, or giving up, our expectations.

Let me give a few examples. You want to go for a walk and leave your phone at home so you are distraction free. You do, only to return home to an angry spouse because you've been gone for two hours, and she has been worried about you.

To avoid the conflict, communicate your expectations:

> You: "Hey babe, I need to clear my thoughts away from texts, calls, and emails, so I'm going to leave my phone here while I go out for a couple of hours."
>
> Your spouse: "No problem. I was going to have dinner on the table in an hour and a half. Can you be home by then?"

> You: "Yes, see you then. Thank you."

By communicating your expectations, you avoid hurting each other.

Here's another example. Last week you and your spouse argued about the way she never cleans up after herself. The conversation went something like this:

> You: "What's the matter with you! You leave your clothes everywhere. You can never find your keys because you put them in a different spot every time you walk in this dang house. You always say, 'I will clean it up later,' and you secretly hope I'll do it! I'm sick of cleaning up for you. I'm not doing it anymore." A tear slowly rolls down his face.
>
> Your spouse: "That's fine. I don't mind living in a mess. Besides, I thought cleaning was your job!"

After a lot of other ridiculous exchanges, you decide to have a healthier conversation that isn't filled with always and never statements—which can't possibly be true and usually lead to more frustration. You reset and calm down, then carefully ask your spouse if you can have a do over, then you have this conversation instead.

> You: "It's important to me that we both clean. We're a team, and I don't mind cleaning up after you every once in a while, but would you make cleaning up after yourself a priority because it's important to me?"
>
> Your spouse: "I hear what you're saying, and I'll work on it, but right now I have some bad habits that probably won't change instantly. Please, remind me and be gracious with me, as I make these changes."
>
> You: "What can I do to help?"

> Your spouse: "Honestly, the best thing you can do to help is clean up after me with a better attitude. Thanks."

Okay, that last part is a joke, but you see how the tone can change so the two of you come out on the same team. Communicate your expectations and create solutions together. Throw out the old scripts so changes can be made.

By the way, about ten years ago, a friend gave me a tip about keeping track of my keys, and I haven't lost my keys since. Put a brightly colored piece of paper on the counter by the front door (or whatever door you enter through when you arrive home). When you walk into the house, empty your pocket onto the paper: keys, change, receipts, pocket lint. Everything goes right there, on the paper. Do that for thirty days, and it will become a habit—a good one.

Unboxing A New Deck of Cards

I use a new deck of cards every time I perform to give me the optimal amount of success in fooling others. Every once in a while, I'm handed a deck of cards with the line, "Can you do something with my deck?" Of course I can, but your deck has spaghetti on it from a meal from six years ago, the corners are completely bent, and the cards stick together. So I answer, "Yes, I can do something with your deck. I can throw it away." Okay, I would never say that. And yes, I can do some mind-blowing illusions with an old deck of cards, but I do my best work with a new one.

In our marriages we can grow stale in our sex life, mundane in our gift giving, boring in our dating, and stagnant in our friendship. However, just like a brand-new deck of cards, we can create a new, vibrant, and fresh marriage every day.

In Christ, every day can be made new. Second Corinthians 4:16–17 reminds us, "Do not lose heart. Though outwardly we are wasting away, yet inwardly we are being renewed day by day. For our light and momentary troubles are achieving for us an eternal glory that far outweighs them all." It's easy to lose heart, to give up, and to resume where we left off yesterday. Daily, we get knocked down. Daily, we're wasting away. But God reminds us that on the inside we're being renewed.

God gives us a fresh start each day. In other words, we can have a new marriage every day, because we're being renewed daily. Not satisfied with the marriage you had yesterday? Guess what—today is a new day to create the marriage of your dreams. If your struggles and your pain seem endless, this passage reminds us that they are temporary. If we keep our sights set on eternity, God will give us hope for today.

Here's a simple way to put new-day thinking into practice. If you went to bed holding a grudge because your spouse didn't put away the laundry like you asked or take out the trash because it's their "job," you are the one who needs to make a change. In order for every day to start out fresh, we have to bring up any grievances as they occur. (See 1 Corinthians 13:5.)

God's Word says that it's to our benefit to overlook an offense (see Proverbs 19:11). So, if your spouse leaves the recycling piled high in the garage (when they typically are pretty good about taking it out), then maybe you should overlook that offense. The goal is to recognize that their action disappointed you, but you can forgive because you know you forget to do chores too. You aren't perfect either. After forgiving, try to move on with your day without any anger or bitterness toward your spouse. Later, if you still feel frustrated, have a conversation with them.

This chapter is titled "Dealing with Hecklers," so don't be a heckler when you share your grievance. Gently tell your spouse that seeing the overflowing recycling bin frustrated you. Say that you tried to get over it, but you weren't able to, so you're bringing it to their attention. Make your feelings clear. Because acts of service is Kimberly's preferred love language, she would say that my leaving the recycling out makes her feel like I don't care about her.

Equally important is the response to the person bringing up the grievance. If your spouse has come to you and shared something you did, or didn't do, that bothered them, your response is crucial. You don't have to fully understand or agree with their frustration, but you do need to listen to them so they feel heard, then apologize and ask them how you can make changes for next time.

Getting Rid of Unnecessary Cards

Most people aren't even aware that the first thing they do when they open a deck of cards is remove the advertising cards. It's obvious that these don't belong in the deck, so they throw them away.

We can easily fill our marriages with unnecessary cards (pointing out a spouse's faults, lack of forgiveness, keeping score, spying, constant comparing), and if we don't remove them, they put a wedge between us and our spouse.

Ephesians 4:29 reveals three truths that help us discard unnecessary habits: "Do not let any unwholesome talk come out of your mouths, but only what is helpful for building others up according to their needs, that it may benefit those who listen."

KIMBERLY'S CORNER

Our words matter. With them, we have the power to tear each other down or build each other up. In Dr. John Gottman's research of hundreds of couples, he found one of the major predictors of divorce is contempt—making someone else feel beneath you. We have all had someone call us names or say mean things about us, but treating your spouse that way is unacceptable.

No matter how angry you are with your loved one, you are not better than they are, and you have no right to hurt them. Decide right now to stop tearing down your husband or wife.

Don't allow contempt to be part of your relationship. You can do it!

First, determine to have zero tolerance for unwholesome talk coming out of your mouth. The Greek word for unwholesome is *sapros,* which means rotten or unfit for use.[2] The same word is used in Matthew 7:17–18 to refer to rotten fruit and in Matthew 13:48 to talk about rotten fish. Our words should not produce rotten fruit or revolting fish—foods unfit for consumption.

We can justify so much that we say and do, but God calls us to a higher standard. Instead of justifying our hurtful words or actions, we need to admit we have a problem and adjust our words and actions to fall in line with God's instructions.

Second, look for how you can constantly build up your spouse, not according to your needs, but theirs. What does your spouse need? How can you build them up? How can you encourage and empower them to be who God has called them to be?

Finally, building up your spouse doesn't only benefit your relationship, but it also benefits everyone around you—your children, your friends, and your family. In other words, the way in which you speak to your spouse impacts everyone you know. It's that important.

Kimberly and I made a commitment to always speak about each other with love and respect. It would be easy to follow the culture and tear down my wife when she isn't around, but by building her up in these situations, I demonstrate my love for her. When you and your spouse commit to building each other up with your words, you take your love to another level.

Be Prepared

I frequently open my show by tossing a deck of cards into the audience so someone can open and shuffle it. Sometimes, when the person throws the deck of cards back to me, the box opens, and cards go everywhere—like card confetti. What if I wasn't ready with another deck of cards? What if at that point I made people pick up the cards before continuing with the magic? During a show, that would be a major waste of time

However, because I've done thousands of shows, I know it's highly possible that a deck will fall to the floor, have a drink spilled on it, or come back with some middle school boy's gum stuck to the back, so I have extra decks ready for almost any scenario.

In our marriages, we need to prepare for conflict when we aren't fighting. Instead of allowing the same arguments to creep in again and again, we can have a healthy conversation *before an argument starts.* That way, we are prepared to handle the situation with grace, love, and forgiveness.

For example, let's say one of the secrets that rose to the surface after you read chapter 2 was that you've been hiding money from your spouse. To break this cycle of hiding cash, you talk about alternatives together.

> "What if we create a new savings account solely for you?"
>
> "I like the sound of that. What if we create one for you too? That way you have some fun money."
>
> "What about a piggy bank we break open once a year? That way, we don't know how much money is in there. So, it's a secret—our secret!"
>
> "What if we call that piggy bank my purse and you just shove cash in there!"

You see how the conversation has gone from secret stash to creating a future together. We have moved from a secret that hinders to a conversation that opens possibilities.

Your turn. What can you do now that would have a massive payoff in dealing with conflict down the road? Could you and your spouse go to a marriage conference? Could you get away for a weekend? Could you start budgeting so you don't have the same fight about having no money? Could you start dating weekly? How you prepare now will have a massive impact on what you experience later.

The Trick That Can't Be Explained

A trick created by Dai Vernon became legendary. It's called The Trick That Can't Be Explained. Vernon borrowed a deck of cards and asked a spectator to shuffle it. He asked the shuffler to name any card, and Vernon never touched the deck. He then asked the shuffler to turn over the top card of the deck. It was always the named card!

Stop. Reread that. Seriously, think about that. It's amazing!

That's exactly what happened—occasionally. You see, Vernon's trick was that there was a one in fifty-two chance that the card the spectator named was the one on top. That's how his trick became legendary! When the named card wasn't on top, Dai had fifty-one ways to make another magical solution a reality. For example, he could say, "Shuffle the cards as much as you like. I won't ever touch the cards." When the person finished shuffling, Vernon simply said, "Now turn over the top card," and the person screamed in disbelief as their card stared them in the face. This was the one in a million (actually one in fifty-two) that made this trick legendary. The other fifty-one ways that weren't quite as impossible made the legend possible.

When it comes to conflict, you need fifty-one ways to resolve the issues, de-escalate the problems, and bring peace. But one way will create legendary results. One way will make for a better story. One solution isn't possible every time, but when it happens, you remember it because you know your actions reflect what God wants from us every time. Here it is:

> Finally, all of you, be like-minded, be sympathetic, love one another, be compassionate and humble. Do not repay evil with evil or insult with insult. On the contrary, repay evil with blessing, because to this you were called so that you may inherit a blessing. (1 Peter 3:8–9)

Implementing these verses into your marriage is a game changer. If, as a married couple, you are like-minded, sympathetic, loving, compassionate, humble, and you repay insults and evil with blessing, your marriage will be full of *wow!*

Let's break the verse down and think about how great your marriage will be if each component is a regular part of your relationship.

> **Like-minded**. You both have the goal of bringing glory to God and creating a thriving marriage.
>
> **Sympathetic**. You genuinely care deeply about the other person and seek to understand their side of every issue.
>
> **Loving**. You love your spouse not only in words but in actions—in a sacrificial, selfless way.
>
> **Compassionate**. This word comes from the Latin word *compati,* which means to suffer with.[3] When your spouse suffers or hurts, you hurt too.
>
> **Humble**. You position yourself below, not above your spouse—as a servant, not a master. (See Philippians 2:1–8.)

Finally, when your spouse says something hurtful or painful or even nasty, you learn to respond with words that build up, encourage, love, and bless your spouse. You don't escalate the situation by repaying insult with insult.

Repaying evil with good is not what either you or your spouse deserves; this is what God calls you to do for your enemies, so how much more for the person you married! The miracle of Christ working in you is learning to respond to evil and insults with love and blessing. For example, when your spouse says something about your driving, you choose your response. Will you speak in love and with blessing? What about when your spouse doesn't do the dishes and you wake up to a messy kitchen? This is another opportunity to show love and to bless, to hear their side of the story. Every day God gives us countless opportunities to respond with kindness, love, and blessing, but it's usually a choice that goes against our knee-jerk response.

A Little-Known Secret

For decades I've studied efficiency and tried to understand how to maximize my productivity. I came to faith in Christ when I was seventeen years old and started reading through the Bible for the first time. One day I read Mark 1:35—"Very early in the morning, while it was still dark, Jesus got up, left the house and went off to a solitary place, where he prayed." My teenage brain concluded that if it was important to Jesus to wake early, it should be important to me too. To this day, I wake up early. I believe this gives me a significant advantage on tackling the problems of the day through prayer and reading God's Word before the challenges of family, work, and life come my way.

There is no tangible way for me to prove the effectiveness of prayer and daily Bible study, but I believe that this one habit—waking up early to connect with God—has equipped me to fight for my marriage, my family, and my work.

The time of day doesn't matter. The key is carving out time to pray and read God's Word daily. One famous Christian writer is well-known for his all-night prayer and Bible reading habits because he hates getting up early!

The point is that we need God's input in our lives and in our marriages. If we want to avoid being hecklers who point out the faults of our spouses and instead become people who encourage, forgive, reconcile, and love like Jesus, we need God's help. And whether you meet Him early in the morning, catch up with Him at lunch, or find Him after the kids are down for the night, He is always ready to meet with you.

CREATING MAGIC TOGETHER

TAKEAWAY

Trying to be like-minded, sympathetic, loving, compassionate, and humble to your mate is a tall order. However, if you do that, you will encourage and bless him or her.

QUESTIONS

1. What can I change in my tone or language to be a better spouse?
2. Is there any area that is painful to talk about because of the way I respond to you?
3. How can we make sure we create a new future and not return to the old patterns?

PLAN OF ACTION

Take turns discussing a time when you felt love and kindness from you mate. Talk about ways that situation could have gone differently, and make a promise to be conscious of new ways to keep showing love, kindness, and respect to each other.

MIND-BLOWING BEDROOM MAGIC

A Magician's Guide to Sex

Adam and his wife were both naked, and they felt no shame.

—Genesis 2:25

One unique thing about traveling is where you stay the night. If I were working for corporate America, I might stay at fancy hotels. Since most of my work involves faith-based ministries, I've had different kinds of doors opened—literally. I've enjoyed sleeping in epic hotel rooms, but I've also slept in dorm rooms, barns, on living room couches and empty floors, in trailers and even seedy motels where the person before you left their cigarettes on the bed and the housekeeping staff didn't clean it up.

Working with churches often leads to a memorable homestay. Lots of people who love Jesus want to open their homes to strangers like me. They all have great intentions, and some homestays have been the best experiences. Others were, well … interesting.

The following story ranks with one of my most awkward homestays, and some of the details have been changed to protect identities.

When I arrive at an event location, most of the time I've been awake since 3:30 a.m., and I've hauled my luggage through two or three airports. So I can be tired when I reach my final destination.

This particular time, I arrived at the home of a large family. Each member of the family had their predetermined chair to sit on at mealtime. One person kindly brought a bean bag over for me to sit in. I was seven inches lower than everyone else at the table. Awkward! Even the eight-year-old looked down on me.

After a tasty dinner, the mom and dad looked at each other and then at me. All the kids were silent. Awkward. They knew what was coming, but I had no idea. The mom started, "When Pastor Jack asked if someone could house you for the weekend, we knew we had a couch, and we also need help with something, so we said, 'Yes.'"

The dad looked at Alex, their sixteen-year-old son, and said, "Alex. It's okay. I'll ask for you." Turning to me he continued, "Alex has had a hard time meeting girls, and we thought if you taught him a card trick, he could find himself a girl." Awkward.

I taught him a cool trick and talked with him for a while, but in my opinion, Alex had bigger problems than learning a card trick—he needed to learn that magic tricks are rarely the way to a girl's heart. I wanted to say, "Really, you think one trick, *one trick*, is going to land you the girl of your dreams? It took a lot more than magic tricks to win over my wife. In fact, I think she fell for me despite my magic tricks, not because of them."

Similarly, creating magic in the bedroom requires more than having one trick up your sleeve. The ability to create magic in the bedroom demands that you be on top of your game in all areas of communication.

For a lot of couples, talking about sex can be awkward, uncomfortable, embarrassing, or even painful because of past trauma.

> Sex can be scary. Talk about it.
>
> Sex can be painful. Talk about it.
>
> Sex can be fun. Talk about it.

Your spouse is supposed to be your best friend, the one with whom you can share everything and not feel judged. If you don't have that kind of relationship yet, that's okay, but that's still the goal. Being able to voice your sexual needs, desires, fears, and even fantasies is one of the unique aspects of marriage. Sexual intimacy is a special part of the marriage relationship because we don't share that part of our marriage with anyone else, and nothing else is more vulnerable. With sex, you're putting all your cards on the table.

Creating Space for the Conversation

Assuming that no physical ailment prevents you from having sex with your spouse, sexual intimacy is essential to the health of your marriage. Using some of the language we talked about earlier—"this is important to me"—I encourage you to regularly have healthy conversations about your sex life. To do this, make sure you're both in a place where you can hear each other's thoughts and respond in a respectful, loving way.

For some relationships, this can be anywhere, anytime. If that's not your marriage, go to a place away from kids or other distractions and give yourself time to dive deep into this conversation.

Some of the questions you might ask are:

> Does talking about sex make you uncomfortable? Why?
>
> How can we learn to be more intimate in our sex life?
>
> Do you have any fears about sex? How can I help alleviate any of those fears?
>
> Are you satisfied with our sex life?
>
> What do you think we can do to improve our sex life?
>
> What's something new we could try in the bedroom? (always staying within the context of marriage)

Positions Matter

I love magic books. They've been my primary source of learning the craft of magic for decades. One thing I find fascinating is that most authors assume everyone has the same size hands and can do moves or sleights the way they are taught in the books. However, I have often found that I need to hold the deck of cards slightly different to make a particular move work for me. In talking with other magicians, I've learned this is also true for almost every one of them—we all have to adapt the move to make it work for us.

The point is, one method may work for one magician but may not for another. This is true in magic, and it is true in the bedroom. We have to adapt, change, and discover what works with our spouse. This is why communication is so important.

You and your spouse have different views on how to handle money, who should be president, and what constitutes a healthy sex life. This shouldn't surprise you. When it comes to sex, talk about it! Discuss what moves work well for you and what you like and don't like. Sex is the most intimate connection with your spouse, so both of you should enjoy it. Together, you are in control of this. You can change your lovemaking from mundane to magical or from painful to beautiful if you talk about it together. Share your likes, dislikes, and fantasies with each other.

Intimacy makes sex magical, and intimacy has far more to do with what happens *outside* the bedroom than inside it. Let's just say, in our house intimacy starts with taking out the trash, doing the dishes, and of course, vacuuming. So, if you want to experience a better sex life, learn to be intimate in all areas of your life, and it will increase your intimacy in the bedroom.

Timing Matters

Couples want to know how often they should be having sex, but no one can say everyone should be doing it X number of times per week.

Everyone has different sex drives, different schedules, and different life situations. Most likely, you and your spouse have different sex drives. If one of you wants it daily and the other wants it every fourteen days, what do you do?

First, recognize that this is by God's design. If we all wanted sex all the time, we would never get anything else done. While we all might be walking around with big smiles on our faces, the bills would pile up as tall as our stack of unfinished work tasks. God uniquely designed us with different desires, and this is good. We tend to use these differences against each other instead of figuring out how to serve, sacrifice, and compromise for each other—which makes us into better people.

Philippians 2:4 says, "Let each of you look not only to his own interests, but also to the interests of others" (ESV). How can we apply this to sex in our marriage? How can we look to our spouse's interest? How can we compromise without giving in on the one hand or feeling rejected on the other? How can you give instead of take?

The key is to find the right balance that serves your needs and desires as well as the desires and needs of your spouse. Talk about different ways you can give each other the hint that you are in the mood for sex. Talk about how you can gently tell your spouse no if it's not going to happen that day.

When Kimberly and I first got married, we had a vicious cycle or script that went like this: "Do you want to do it?" "No babe, not tonight." Then dead silence, pain, hurt, and rejection ensued. We wasted so much time focused on our own hurts and not wanting to compromise, because we didn't understand each other's actual needs and desires.

She confesses that early on, she had no idea that my desire to be intimate with her more frequently was part of the way God designed me. She says that understanding how differently we are wired truly helped her, which in turn helped our sex life. On the flip side, I also learned that her saying no to sex was not an intentional rejection of me; neither was it a prison sentence of no sex forever.

Scheduled Sex

When our sons were toddlers, life looked a lot different than it does now. We were often running on fumes, especially as we were also launching our ministry during that season. The hormone changes from having children can decrease your wife's sex drive along with the sheer exhaustion that comes from being needed 24/7 while children are young. Kimberly and I knew that sex still had to be a part of our lives, but it was hard to find times that we both desired physical intimacy.

During that season, we found scheduled sex to be an effective way to make sure we were meeting each other's sexual needs. This simply meant that we talked about a day (or days) each week where we would make time to make love. Yes, she even put a little heart on the calendar for those days so we both knew it was going to happen.

KIMBERLY'S CORNER

1 Corinthians 7:3–6 reminds us to give ourselves as a gift to our spouse. The author, Paul, talks about couples not depriving each other and about self-control.

This idea of sex being a gift to each other has really helped me to say yes more often and has caused me to initiate more often too. My husband works hard, and I know how much he loves me. When I keep that at the forefront of my mind, it's easier to give him the most vulnerable part of myself. The bedroom is a place where you can be naked in front of each other, and the intimate bond you can create there is magical if you let down your defenses. This is an experience you shouldn't have with anyone else, so be giving to each other, making sure it's a pleasurable experience for both of you.

Lovemaking should be a regular part of your marriage, so if it's not, talk to each other and find a way to make a change.

She gave me hope! Those hearts took away the guesswork for me, and although I continued to woo her, at least I knew which days were going to lead to something physical. I know a schedule takes all the spontaneity out of sexual intimacy, but the hearts on the calendar gave me hope and meant that my advances toward her would not end in rejection. Scheduled sex helped us both during that season of life.

Maybe you're in a season that you can be more spontaneous in your sex life. Those are fun times. Enjoy them. Sometimes my wife takes me to a hotel for a "lunch break." Other times we just give each other that look and it's on! However, spontaneity can be tricky, and you need to know your spouse well so you can discern when it's a great time and when it's not. Asking questions like "What would be the ideal conditions for spontaneous sex?" would put the two of you on the same page for more unplanned sex.

You and your spouse can also agree on a visual cue. For example, if I put the blinds down while looking at Kimberly's dreamy eyes and she winks at me, she's saying, "This is happening!" But if I pull the blinds down and she puts on her snowsuit, I know what that means too.

Dealing with Rejection

When I was fifteen years old, I tried out for the world-famous Magic Castle's junior membership program. My audition went great. The response of the crowd was strong but waiting to see if I was good enough to be among the best was stressful.

Finally, the letter arrived, but the words on the page were not the ones I hoped to read: "We regret to inform you ..." That letter of rejection stayed in my head for years. It pushed me to work harder, to strive to be even better, but no matter how many times someone said, "Your magic is amazing," the loudest voice was still "You're not good enough."

Kimberly and I have worked with a lot of couples over the years, and a common refrain is a struggle with being turned down in the bedroom. The feeling of rejection can lead to anger, frustration, and division in your marriage. Sex becomes a tool or a weapon that spouses use against each other instead of an intimate act that draws them closer together.

I've had to learn that Kimberly isn't withholding or using sex as a bargaining chip or some power move; sometimes she is too exhausted, not in the mood, or simply doesn't want to do it. And that's okay. She isn't rejecting me or saying, "That is never going to happen!" On her side of it, she has learned to give me hope (by giving me a time in the near future), or she has chosen to engage when she isn't feeling it and reminds me that she's for our marriage! Sex is a marriage issue, and she wants our marriage to thrive in every area.

Using a Scale

Kimberly and I use a scale for quite a few things in our marriage but not the scale you step on to find out your weight. On the contrary, she admits she hates that kind of scale. Rather, we use a rating scale. For example, on a scale of one to ten, how are you feeling? For us, one is "I feel like I'm going to die." A ten is "I feel fantastic!"

On a scale of one to ten, how are you feeling about going out tonight? One means "No thank you. I really want to stay under a blanket and snuggle." Ten means "I need out for my own sanity." Even though it's a little tricky, we sometimes use this scale in the bedroom. On a scale of one to ten, do you want to have sex right now? One means, "Not a chance." Ten means "I'm ripping off all my clothes. I'm ready!"

The problem is, I'm always at a ten.

If she wakes me up in the middle of the night. That's a perfect ten!

I'm exhausted from work. Well, let's finish well. I'm a ten.

I'm sick, but I'm sure sex is the cure. I'm ready. Ten.

We just got into a huge fight. Haven't you heard of makeup-sex? Ten.

My wife, on the other hand, is all over the map. Sometimes she's a one, or a seven, or sometimes a three, then sometimes she's a ten. I never know when or where or how it happens that she moves to a ten; however, I've learned that cleaning any part of the house definitely tips the scale in the right direction.

The truth is that she's simply more complex than I am. God designed us in different ways. Genesis 2:24–25 says, "Therefore a man shall leave his father and his mother and hold fast to his wife; and they shall become one flesh. And the man and his wife were both naked and were not ashamed" (ESV).

God designed men and women in vastly different ways, but His desire is that we become one with our spouse, learning to be naked and unashamed. So, pleasure isn't our primary goal; rather we should be pursuing intimacy (in every way) with our spouse.

The Reset Button

This is probably not true for everyone, but sex can be like hitting a Reset button on your marriage. Some couples are stuck in a horrible cycle of one person wanting to be physically intimate, but the other person withholding sex because they want their spouse to earn it, or they are holding grudges and keeping score. Sometimes, the physical act of love-making can bring a couple together and help them reset and wipe the scoreboard clean again.

Science proves this. "When we are intimate with someone, oxytocin, also known as the 'love hormone,' is released into the body during intercourse and other forms of intimacy," says Dr. Sal Raichbach, a psychologist and licensed clinical social worker. She also adds, "Oxytocin is linked to positive social functioning and is associated with bonding, trust and loyalty."[4] Sex can release tension between the two of you. Sex can create emotional and spiritual connection. Sex can help the two of you to be back on the same page.

Creating magic in the bedroom is a game changer for marriages. A healthy sex life is often a barometer for every area of your marriage, so talk about intimacy and work toward being naked and unashamed.

If your sex life isn't currently what you wish it was, that's okay. Sit down and think about what you could do to make sex more enjoyable for your partner. Then talk to your partner and share with them that you would like to make this part of your marriage better. You could be looking for more frequency, more foreplay, or any number of things. The goal is to discover great intimacy while bringing mutual enjoyment and serving each other best. Think in terms of a win-win. Learning to meet your spouse's needs in the bedroom will create magic in your marriage.

CREATING MAGIC TOGETHER

TAKEAWAY

Order dinner in and talk about your sex life. Just talk.

QUESTIONS

1. What's going great? What's not?
2. What are solutions to create more intimate times together?

PLAN OF ACTION

Initiate sex and do something different. (It doesn't have to be a big difference. Maybe a different time of day—or let your imagination fly. But make sure it's something you'll both enjoy.)

SECTION 2

SECRETS TO OVERCOMING THE IMPOSSIBLE

Remember Dai Vernon's illusion called The Trick That Can't Be Explained? (See chapter 5.) When I was twelve years old, I worked on that trick nonstop until I had removed every obstacle and could find each card effortlessly. I was relentless.

When we approach obstacles in our marriage with the mentality that there is always a way around, over, or through them, we'll be saying, "My spouse is amazing. You wouldn't believe what we have overcome. I know we look like we don't have any problems, but that's not the case. We have learned to overcome them, together."

In Psalm 18:28-29, David reminds us of who God is and what He has the power to do in our lives. He says, "You, LORD, keep my lamp burning; my God turns my darkness into light. With your help I can advance against a troop; with my God I can scale a wall."

"But God, being rich in mercy, because of the great love with which he loved us, even when we were dead in our trespasses, made us alive together with Christ—by grace you have been saved" (Ephesians 2:4–5

ESV). The two words at the beginning of verse four change everything for our marriages. God interrupts our pain, our challenges, and our failures with "but God" showed up and revealed His mercy and love to bring us together!

What if "but God" became the mantra for your marriage?

I feel like I'm burning out, but God keeps my lamp burning.

I feel like the darkness is winning, but God turns my darkness into light.

The odds are stacked against us, but God helps to keep us moving forward against the troops (the struggles, the obstacles to peace).

The walls are closing in around us, but God helps us to scale the impossible walls in front of us.

We need to look at obstacles as challenges, not as impassable blockades. Obstacles are opportunities to show character, and they give us the chance to love our spouse in deep, meaningful ways. Many obstacles can't be avoided, but they can be overcome as we live out our faith and seek to give glory to God.

We can choose to focus on what's possible rather than what seems impossible. We lay out those apparent impossibilities and present them, in prayer, to God. We ask God to help us overcome the impossible situations in which we find ourselves. My prayer is that you and your spouse will look at obstacles, struggles, and conflict in a new way.

Challenges are opportunities to bring glory to God in the middle of life's storms. In this section, we'll look at how to overcome the obstacles that are holding us back from a better marriage.

When the odds are stacked against your marriage, when the giants are bigger than you expected, when the battle to keep your love thriving is harder than you imagined, when the fears seem too big to handle: God is bigger. God is deeply invested in your marriage and wants you to succeed.

Do you ever feel like the problems in your marriage are too big and the work to fix them won't be worth the effort? You've tried everything but find yourself at the same dead end. You're sick of trying to fix the problems because nothing seems to work.

I'm sorry you've felt this pain and hopelessness. What if I told you there was a way out, a way to make your marriage better? Would you believe me? Our beliefs determine our actions.

Are you ready to start seeing obstacles in a new light? Let's become relentless, like a twelve-year-old wannabe magician learning a legend's trick!

SMOKE AND MIRRORS

The Illusions of Fear

Do not be afraid, little flock, for your Father has been pleased to give you the kingdom.

—Luke 12:32

The concept of smoke and mirrors dates to 1770 when charlatans pretended they could communicate with the dead. Using a hidden projector known as the magic lantern along with a mirror and smoke, the swindlers convinced their marks that they were seeing a ghost. Can you imagine how convincing that would have been 350 years ago? (Who am I kidding? It would probably still fool audiences.) People genuinely believed that what they were seeing was a real ghost—maybe a relative who had recently died.

Today, the concept of smoke and mirrors is alive and well. The biggest charlatan trying to create a life-altering illusion today is fear. Fear stands tall in our marriages, trying to defeat us and to remind us that we are not enough. Fear tells us we are not loved, and it is trying to control our thoughts and actions.

All of us have different fears, but we don't want our fears to drive the actions we take in our marriage. When fear gets the best of us, we become less proactive and more reactive. When fear takes over, God appears small and distant instead of bigger and more intimate than we can imagine. Ultimately, fear makes our pain, our struggles, and our problems—projected over a cloud of smoke—seem more real than the love, grace, and forgiveness of God.

Some of you are probably dealing with the reality that you live with a spouse who doesn't love you or one who maybe wants out of the marriage. That's not a fear; it's a reality. But you still don't want fear to drive your decisions; prayer and love need to be the center point for your choices.

KIMBERLY'S CORNER

A friend of ours, Joe Castañeda, says, "If it's not an option, it won't be." In other words, if something is not an option or a possibility, then it cannot come to pass.

The day you were married, the word *divorce* should be removed from your thoughts and your vocabulary. If both parties truly commit to never getting divorced, then every marriage challenge has a solution. The question then becomes am I going to have a happy marriage or a miserable marriage? If you currently have a miserable marriage, I'm willing to bet it's not only because of the other person. You have a role in it and have contributed to the misery. So what can you do now?

I propose you both decide to put to death the old ways of your old marriage and start anew, together. It might be scary, but if you can't do this, you're probably holding on too tight to the pain of the past, and essentially you aren't choosing a happy marriage. Danny and I have seen God change some awful marriages. I know it can be scary, but all you have to do right now is be willing to try.

The insights I share in this chapter assume that you and your spouse want and are willing to make the necessary changes to bring healing and hope into your marriage.

Fears That Paralyze Us

Every day you and your spouse deal with unknown pressures. Mounting pressures lead to disconnection, disconnection leads to suspicion and an overall lack of trust, and a lack of trust leads us to our biggest marital fears. These fears can easily drive you apart. On the other hand, dealing with them can lead to deeper trust in your marriage.

Fears have many triggers. Here are a few:

Your spouse heads off to work. Will a conversation lead to flirtation and flirtation lead to emotional detachment and emotional detachment to an affair? The thoughts lead us spiraling into a pit of despair and anxiety.

Maybe a lot of cash is exchanged in your business, and you're concerned that your spouse will spend some of it on personal shopping.

Maybe you fear that the occasional beer or glass of wine will turn into a six-pack or bottle-a-day, and then a drink in the hand all the time.

Your fears might not even have anything to do with your spouse. Maybe you have insecurity about your appearance or job performance; maybe the crushing stress of daily life has you frozen in old patterns.

Maybe your fear of the unknown involves whether your spouse can really love you because you have a hard time loving yourself. Or you may think that if you start revealing your secrets, your spouse couldn't love you after learning what you've done in the past.

Whatever your fears, the key is that as a couple, you don't operate your life based on your reaction to those fears. Fear-based decisions lead to more failures than successes. Most fears are not based in reality but on what our mind has built up into its own reality. Fear of failure, fear of repeating the history of our parents, fear of falling out of love, and fear of loss are almost always rooted in unknown outcomes. These fears are not from God. In fact, God is pursuing you to remind you that He is for you and stands with you to eliminate fears.

When I was eighteen years old, fears of the unknown—"What's next?" and "What am I going to do with my life?"—circled around and around in my brain. But that cycle would change (or so I thought) when the opportunity of a lifetime came my way. I met a world-renowned magician at one of my shows. After my performance, he told me that he would soon be traveling to Caesar's Palace in Las Vegas, then on to New York, and finally on a tour throughout Europe. "I want you to go with me, Danny," he said. "I will train you, show you the ropes, and show you what it takes to be a world-class magician." Finally, I thought, this is someone who believes in me.

I was so excited. This was a dream come true. Just one snag. One year earlier, I had started a different pursuit. I decided to follow Jesus in every area of my life. So, I prayed about the opportunity offered by this magician and felt God nudging me in a different direction. He was gently moving me away from what I thought was a dream come true. I don't know how to explain it, but I knew God was saying, "No."

I called the magician and told him, "Thank you for the amazing offer, but right now I can't do it." Trust me. Sometimes embracing God's mystery isn't easy. Sometimes it's downright hard, and we don't even know why we are getting a no. But even then, I knew God's dream for me was better than my dream.

God had a better, broader perspective, so I trusted Him as I let go of that dream. About six months later, I started volunteering in the youth ministry at my church. Over the next ten years, I volunteered, interned, and after graduating from seminary, I became the youth pastor there. I loved doing youth ministry in the local church, but different people challenged me to step out and combine my ability to do illusions with my passion to share God's love with people.

At that time, I was far more interested in continuing youth ministry. That is, until I read a verse that shook me to my core. It changed everything. Romans 11:29 says, "God's gifts and his call are irrevocable." That was the first time I saw calling and gifting intertwined, inseparable from each other. I knew I had to combine these two loves into one ministry.

About a month after reading that passage, I was at the local gym in desperate need of something to distract me from the rigors of my workout. I picked up a magazine I don't normally read and started leafing haphazardly through the pages. Soon I saw the smiling picture of the magician I had met ten years earlier. Even though I hadn't seen him or even thought about that day for years, I recognized him right away.

As I read the article, I found out that he was on trial for multiple counts of fraud. He had been a great magician and had used his skills to get bookings all over the world. However, he invited college students to go on tour with him and then asked them to use their credit cards for his traveling expenses. He explained to them that he would take care of their credit card debt in the next city, but what really happened was that as soon as the students' credit cards had been maxed out, he stranded them in some foreign location. He literally abandoned these young adults all over the world.

I realized with 100-percent certainty that he would have used and abandoned me if I had gone with him. If I had not listened to God's voice guiding me, I would have been stranded, penniless, knowing no one in a country where English probably wasn't spoken, and wondering how I would get home to my family.

That day at the gym I realized how much listening to God's voice mattered. For me, age eighteen wasn't the right time to start doing magic full-time. Becoming a magician at that point would have been far more about me and less about glorifying God. It would have been about me trying to fit into the world's plan for me and not waiting on God's plan for me. God had to shape me, teach me, and prepare me for a worldwide ministry. God had laid the foundation for me to start a new ministry of sharing God's life-changing message through captivating illusions.

Whether or not your fears are based in reality, that doesn't change the power of who God is and the choice that we have to be obedient to His Word: "Fear not." I know, easier said than done.

When the disciples were in the middle of a storm, waves were crashing into the boat, and they literally thought they had seen a ghost and fully believed they were going to die. While they feared the end of their lives was near, where was Jesus? Taking a nap in the boat. Seriously, check out the story in Mark 4:35–41.

This story leads to some questions: Doesn't God care about our storms? Does He sleep through our biggest anxieties and fears? When we cry out to God, does He sleep through our screams, our pain, and our suffering? Do we have to wake Jesus for Him to calm the storms of our lives?

For the disciples, three words changed the outcome of the storm. Out of fear, the disciples woke up Jesus. After looking around, He spoke to the wind and waves and said, "Quiet! Be still!" (Mark 4:39).

To answer our questions, let's look at what Jesus said a few moments before He and His disciples got into the boat. He said, "Let us go over to the other side" (Mark 4:35). With the storm raging around them, the disciples forgot Jesus had told them where they were going. In other words, they were not going to die in the storm.

Think about your marriage. How did God speak to you before you got into the storm? What was life like before you started seeing barriers? Can you clearly remember anything God told you?

Sometimes, like the disciples, we forget that Jesus isn't going to leave us all alone. We're going to get through this together. We're going to get to the other side of the storm.

Does God hear our cries in the midst of our suffering? Yes.

In the midst of our pain? Yes.

In the midst of our cries? Yes.

Psalm 56:8 says that God keeps track of our sorrows and holds our tears in a jar. He does know, and He does care enough to catalog our heartache. God is with you in every season of life, even ones of deep sorrow.

But do we—do you—cling to His promises and believe Him at His word?

After calming the sea, Jesus asked His followers a powerful question: "Why are you so afraid?" (Mark 4:40). The answer seems simple, right? The storm scared them because the waves were about to capsize the boat and they were going to drown.

The storm was real, but the fear of dying was smoke and mirrors. In our marriages, we have to learn to distinguish between the storms that are real and the fear that is paralyzing us.

The Way Out

To live fearlessly seems impossible, yet God wants us to live fearlessly in our marriages. One verse helped me learn how to live without fear. These seventeen words can change your life because fear will no longer get the best of you. This single verse is the way out of every fear you will ever have.

When your fears are about to get the best of you, think of this verse and draw strength from its truth. Jesus gives us deep insight into how to deal with fear: "Do not be afraid, little flock, for your Father has been pleased to give you the kingdom" (Luke 12:32).

Jesus starts out with a command "do not be afraid." But the next part gives us insight into why we don't need to fear. Jesus says that we are His "little flock." Why should that comfort us? Because God is so big. We are small compared to our Shepherd. If we are part of His flock, we know He is our Shepherd. The Shepherd will guide and direct us.

Jesus goes on to say, "For your Father has been pleased." There are two truths to wrestle through here. One, you don't need to fear because your heavenly Father is perfect and loves you. Your heavenly Father has the power to protect, comfort, and care for you.

The second is a little trickier and might be a harder pill for some of us to swallow. Your Father "has been pleased" with you. For some of us, it's hard to imagine a God that is pleased with us. We have terrible memories and images of a father, and we can't imagine one that is pleased with us.

These thoughts lead us into a cycle of trying to please that constantly leaves us coming up short. We try to earn God's approval and grace, but this repetition has caused tremendous pain for you and for your spouse.

I want you to hear it again. God is pleased with you. Not pleased because of what you've done. Not pleased because of your accomplishments. He is pleased because you are His child. Your existence, by being who you are, brings Him joy.

He is pleased with you.

Finally, Jesus says, "To give you his kingdom." If God is inviting you into His kingdom, then we know that He is a King. The King has the authority to cast out fear. The King helps us overcome. The King has the power to set us free. God is inviting you to be a part of His kingdom, His story. When, as a couple you say yes to the King, you will discover the marriage He has designed for you.

The next time fears creep in, take comfort in the knowledge that you have a great Shepherd, a loving Father, and an all-powerful King. You don't need to fear because God is your Shepherd, your Father, and your King. The way out of fear is to shift your focus to God and know that His plan for your marriage is bigger than your plan and He is pleased with you.

Over the years, I've done numerous escapes. Underwater escapes, hangman's noose, buried alive, straitjackets, and many more. One time, when I was nailed shut in a coffin, I couldn't figure out how to escape, and I was losing oxygen. My slow-intentional-controlled breathing was waning, and I knew if I lost consciousness, my life was over. I needed a solution fast.

The voices of fear, failure, death, and humiliation were louder than the voice reminding me to rely on my training, knowledge, and preparation. I almost let my fears win, but then this thought got stuck in my head: There's always a way out. There's always a way out. There's always a way out!

Whatever struggles your marriage might have, God is your shepherd, your Father, and your king. He is wise enough to lead you to healing, strong enough to bring you forgiveness, and loving enough to teach you how to restore your marriage. It might seem like you're completely buried, but there is always a way out that leads to a healthier marriage. Always. You might have to try a thousand different ways, but don't give up. God will be with you through it all. With Him, there is always a way.

CREATING MAGIC TOGETHER

TAKEAWAY

What fears are holding you back from becoming the couple God designed you to be? Talk about your fears, listen to each other's stories, and seek to understand your spouse's needs.

Ask each other: "What can I do to help you with your fears?"

QUESTIONS

What situation has left you feeling there is no way out of your marriage? Share that with your spouse and discuss why you feel the situation is so hopeless. Together, pray that God will remove the hopeless feelings and fill you with His hope because of His great love for you.

PLAN OF ACTION

Commit to each other that you will listen to God's still small voice. Share with each other when you hear that voice and pray through the situation together.

8

THINKING OUTSIDE THE BOX

Escaping the Traps of Social Media

Do not be conformed to this world, but be transformed
by the renewal of your mind, that by testing
you may discern what is the will of God,
what is good and acceptable and perfect.

—Romans 12:2 ESV

For centuries, magicians have used trapdoors to convince their audiences that the illusionist can make items disappear or reappear with the snap of his finger or the wave of his wand. The proper use of trapdoors ensures that the audience doesn't suspect, let alone detect, their use.

Social media has a thousand trapdoors that can make great marriages disappear. The pressures of being online and maintaining an online presence can strain marriages in ways never before possible. Whether it's an ex from high school trying to rekindle a relationship, jealousy about other couples who seem to have it all, or reading into something from a picture of your spouse and someone else, these are issues we didn't have before we started logging into Facebook, TikTok, Instagram, and the other platforms available. If we don't deal with it head-on, social media can fracture our marriages.

The relationship between social media and marriage isn't about what's right and wrong as much as it's about creating a healthy marriage by not falling through the trapdoors of social media.

Trapdoors of Social Media

A picture might be worth one thousand words, but how those words are interpreted can build up or tear down a relationship. According to broadbandsearch.net, the average amount of time the global community spends on social media is 144 minutes a day—that's a lot of opportunities to fall through trapdoors.[5] Let's look at a few pitfalls and discover effective strategies to avoid them.

Comparison

If you've spent more than sixty seconds online, you know how easily we can slip into comparing ourselves to the lives of neighbors, friends, and some strangers we follow on social media. Before we know it, we're becoming jealous or spending money trying to keep up with a profile that at best is curated and at worst might be completely false. In our marriages, this can be extremely dangerous, because we might not even be aware that what we're viewing is affecting our self-image, our desires, or our reality. Comparison is a dangerous game, one in which you always come up short and always lose.

I love how Theodore Roosevelt put it: "Comparison is the thief of joy."[6] The quickest way for us to lose the joy God desires for our marriages is to compare our lives and our marriages to those of other people. Proverbs 14:30 says, "A heart at peace gives life to the body, but envy rots the bones."

The antidote for comparison is to learn to be at peace, to be thankful for everything God has given us, and to be content. The Bible reminds us that "godliness with contentment is great gain" (1 Timothy 6:6). This secret is worth living out in your marriage.

Private vs. Public

Another trapdoor is what we put on social media. You might think it's hilarious to post a picture of your spouse sleeping on the couch. Others might think it's funny too, but their opinions mean nothing if your spouse is embarrassed and frustrated that they can't do anything without ending up on social media. This isn't to say that you can't be playful online and put embarrassing stuff out there. But you need to have that conversation with your spouse, and you both should agree on what goes public and what stays private. The goal is to discover what both of you are comfortable putting online.

Wasting Time

A more subtle trapdoor is related to the amount of time we spend on social media. One of the great features on many smart phones is the breakdown of your screen time. In other words, your device can tell you what apps you use the most and how much time you're spending on each one. Most phones even break down time use by app category (sports apps, social media apps, games).

Evaluate what is right for you and how much time is too much. I can't tell you ten minutes a day is the right limit for social media. What I can say is that if our time is limited here on earth, we should want to invest it well. If you spend the global average of 144 minutes a day (check your phone) scrolling your feeds, that's almost seventeen hours a week—over thirty-six days a year spent on social media. That's a lot of time.

Let's not waste our time. Instead, let's make sure that we're using social media and it's not using us. In Ephesians, Paul reminds us that we should "be very careful, then, how you live—not as unwise but as wise, making the most of every opportunity, because the days are evil" (5:15–16). Social media used with wisdom can make a massive impact on God's family. If it's used unwisely, we can end up wasting so much of our lives.

KIMBERLY'S CORNER

Danny and I joke about having thousands of rules in our marriage. From the very beginning, a part of making up after a fight was to talk about a way we could do it differently the next time the issue came up. From there, it became a rule, (e.g., Rule #523: Don't drive away angry).

Okay, we don't actually have the rules numbered, but if we did, the social media rule might be #6519: Do not post without asking. As we grow older, we laugh a little more at ourselves and post sillier pictures. However, we prefer to run something by each other before we post about the family.

Even with the kids, we ask for their permission because they understand that what is put on social media could be in cyberspace forever. So, if they don't think the picture of them is acceptable, then we don't post it. Be mindful of how others might feel about your post. It's not that hard, just be kind.

Self-Deception

I've spent a lifetime learning how deception works, so trust me when I say, people are easily deceived. It can happen with a simple glance. If I go to a park in the middle of the day and look intently at the sky as if I see something, others will look too. The action of looking into the sky deceived them into thinking something interesting was there. A thousand optical illusions can deceive our minds and our eyes. One of my favorites is called The Troxler Effect. This visual deception was discovered in 1804. You stare at an image for about twenty seconds without blinking, and then the image vanishes.

Bizarre, right? Much like this image disappearing from our sight, we can vanish into social media while our spouse longs for that same attention. Let's not deceive ourselves into thinking that social media isn't affecting our relationship with our spouse. If you want to know, ask.

Shallow Relationships

A social media trapdoor many have fallen through opens up when we trust an online relationship. If there's any place that can generate shallow relationships, it's the online world. Cyberspace is full of "I only know it's your birthday because it popped up on my screen," "I'll pray for you," (which means happy thoughts are coming your way or something equally meaningless), and "Let me like your photo while making a snide comment." Again, it's not that you can't have meaningful relationships online, but we have to be intentional to make contact meaningful with the ones we love.

The unfortunate reality for our marriages is that one of our posts can easily draw attention, and soon we find ourselves longing for online attention instead of attention from our spouse. A wife posts a picture of herself as she marches out the door to work, or a husband throws up a mirror selfie after working out at the gym. Within thirty minutes, the photos have garnered a lot of attention, including praise, adoration, and even flirty comments from people of the opposite sex. We then find ourselves craving that attention and even desiring what we perceive are sexy comments from others.

Proverbs 31:30 reminds us that "charm is deceitful and beauty is vain" (ESV). Our pursuit of praise and attention outside of our marriage can have devastating results on our relationships. Instead of seeking those things online, express your need for affirmation and desire to your spouse.

I know my wife needs to hear how much I love her and how beautiful I think she is even on (especially on) days when she doesn't feel it. And she knows that I need to hear, regularly, that she's still attracted to me.

These intentional pursuits can go miles in preventing us from seeking attention from others online. There's a fine line between receiving attention and seeking it; knowing the difference can help you to make healthier social media choices.

The Battle for Focus

On date night, Kimberly and I are always amazed at the way others use cell phones. When we're in a restaurant together, we see couples on their phones the entire time, barely saying a word to each other. We decided a long time ago to set the parameters and expectations before each date. Are we going to be talking about work? Are we going to be talking about the kids? Are we going to be on our phones or not? If we go to a bookstore to meander (which we both enjoy), are we staying together or not? The battle for our attention is fierce. Depending on our date, the answer to these questions vary, but we address the issues ahead of time so we aren't competing with our phones or frustrated by unmet expectations during our time together.

We want to invest deeply in each other's life, but it's difficult to ignore emails, texts, calls, songs, and a thousand other things distracting us from the present. So, we choose to be as distraction free as possible, and we give the gift of our full focus to each other on a regular basis.

Escaping the Traps of Social Media

Social media is neutral. It's not evil, and it's not the problem. It offers incredible amounts of opportunities and information, but it also provides traps into which we can fall. As a couple, evaluate how social media affects your marriage and figure out solutions that work best for you. One of the secrets to discovering what's best for you is found in Romans 12:1–2: "Do not be conformed to this world, but be transformed by the renewal of your mind, that by testing you may discern what is the will of God, what is good and acceptable and perfect" (ESV). Do not become like everyone else on social media—bragging and making every part of your life look great. Ask God to make your mind new so you seek His will for your marriage and avoid wasting your life comparing yourself to others or finding value in what they think of you.

What's God's will? I'm glad you asked. Paul gives us great insight into God's will in nine words and three commands. If we do these three things, we'll be right in the center of God's will. Paul says, "Rejoice always, pray continually, give thanks in all circumstances; for this is God's will for you in Christ Jesus" (1 Thessalonians 5:16–18).

If Paul were living in the era of social media, he may have posted those words on a meme, and it would have gone viral. There would have been thousands of thumbs ups and thousands of thumbs down. Somebody would have commented, "That's a lofty idea, but how can I give thanks when I lost my job today?" Another person would have added, "And I got a call from the doctor saying the unimaginable," or "I broke my ankle on a run today. If that's God's will to say thank you and rejoice in those situations—I'm out."

I get it. I have thought about these verses thousands of times. A while ago, Kimberly and I even printed up bracelets with these verses on them. For years, I wore those verses around my wrist reminding me to rejoice always—not only on the good days but every single day. That bracelet reminded me to pray all the time, day and night, and to give thanks for everything, no matter the circumstances.

So it might come as a surprise to you that when my son Spencer and I found a large rock had been thrown through a window on my wife's vehicle at our hotel in Hesperia, Calif., we didn't post it to social media or try to find justice online. No joke, we prayed and thanked God. I admit that when I called Kimberly at home to tell her what had happened, she was frustrated that we had been vandalized, but how could she be upset when our first response was to thank God? Before calling the police and reporting $7,225 worth of stolen items, my wife, daughter, and oldest son joined us in prayer (over the phone) to thank God for this crazy loss. The bracelet I had worn for years reminded me to pray and give thanks right there and then, for a situation that was less than desirable. That story ends with God showering incredible favor on us. Almost all the items were returned to us (some of them family heirlooms). But even if He hadn't allowed the story to end that way, we still would have been thankful.

We don't get to choose how others operate, especially online. We don't get to pick the outcome. We get to choose to live remarkably in the midst of suffering, in the midst of the unknown. Social media is filled with many unknowns—celebrations you weren't invited to, people passing away, backstabbing, secret messages from a past lover, and invitations to parties with college buddies. Our character is shaped in our online journey, so whether or not the outcome of our social feed is favorable today, we still choose to become the couple God designed us to be through joy, prayer, and thankfulness.

CREATING MAGIC TOGETHER

TAKEAWAY

Talk to your spouse. Have a conversation about social media and find out if you're both on the same page regarding how it's used, when it's used, and how often it's used.

Social media can be a blessing or a curse. It's a great place to keep up with friends but not a place to air your marriage secrets. Social media can intrude on the time you have with your spouse. Establish guidelines for your social media usage and be sure to have more time together than on social media.

QUESTIONS

1. Ask each other: Does it bother you when I am on social media?
2. Do you care what I post?
3. Are there any concerns you have regarding my social media habits? (If the answer to any of these is yes, then work together

on a plan. Commit and help each other; changing habits take time.)

PLAN OF ACTION

Most phones keep track of weekly phone usage and can tell you how much time you spend on social media. Take a look at yours. What do those numbers reflect? Find ways to reduce your phone time and increase your spouse time.

9

LIGHTS. CAMERA. ACTION.

When Porn Takes Center Stage

Can a man scoop fire into his lap
without his clothes being burned?

—Proverbs 6:27

One of my favorite places in the world to perform is the Magic Castle in Hollywood. On any given night, the audience includes a handful of celebrities, some of the world's best magicians, and on rare occasions, the number-one porn star in the world.

One night after one of my four evening performances, a group of guys approached me and said, "Guess who's here?" They said a woman's name that I didn't recognize, then they went on to talk about some of her films. "She's the number-one porn star in the world," one of the guys explained. After saying I didn't recognize her, one of these men gave me his quick analysis of porn. "Porn is like hot sauce. Some like a little, some like a lot. I just happen to like a lot of hot sauce."

Stunned, I said, "I've never heard it put that way."

"I'll be right back," he said. "I'm going to invite her to your show."

And before I could say anything else, he did.

During my show at the Magic Castle, I often use a volunteer's wineglass. In this show, I used a young lady's wineglass because she was sitting in the front row, but of course I found out later that she, in fact, was the porn star the guys had referenced earlier. The performance went fantastic. When I finished the show, I immediately called Kimberly. I did not want her to hear from someone else, "I saw your husband with a porn star last night."

Without giving her any context (and because we can joke around like this), I said, "Hey babe, in full disclosure I want to let you know there was alcohol involved, things got a little blurry, there was a porn star, and it's hard to say exactly what happened. I mean, it went great! Anyways, wanted to let you know."

She retorted, "Really funny, what happened?"

I messed with Kimberly for a bit before giving her the backstory of the guys and the trick performed with the wine glass. I told her that I'd never again look at a bottle of hot sauce the same way.

Our culture loves pornography. To access porn, you used to have to put on clothes, go to a shady part of town, and purchase a magazine or video of some kind. Now you don't even have to roll out of bed. Almost zero effort is required. With the click of a button, anyone can view a billion videos, photos, and erotic stories. Some data suggests that one in seven online searches involves some form of pornography, while others claim that most of the internet is pornography.[7] Who cares! The reality is that pornography is multiplying like magic.

Pornography transcends economic, racial, and spiritual demographics. A thriving multi-billion-dollar industry, pornography has a stranglehold on countless marriages, leaving individuals and couples riddled with guilt, lost time, and hopelessness.

In a relationship, trust can be lost in a million ways, but pornography not only can steal the trust of our spouse but also crush our partner's self-worth. Winning the fight with pornography leads to a path of deeper intimacy with your spouse. To experience freedom, we drag secrets into the ***light***, look through the ***camera*** lens from a different perspective, and move to ***action*** by taking porn from center stage to the trash can where it belongs.

Lights. Camera. Action.

Addiction runs deep in my family—drugs, alcohol, approval, pornography, gambling, and probably a host of other bad habits. My struggles with pornography and sexual abuse are rooted deep in my personal history. Maybe you or your spouse have similar obstacles to overcome, but allowing the trauma to direct you, the shame to overwhelm you, and the addiction to win is the pathway to a life of regrets. God offers us a road map to healing from past pain, regaining marital intimacy, and finding hope for your marriage.

Your journey to freedom starts by bringing the struggle to light. Have an honest conversation with your spouse about pornography. If this is too difficult or volatile for your relationship, have the conversation with a friend, pastor, or counselor. Specifically talk about the ways pornography hinders you from having the best possible marriage.

Let me make a point by being ridiculous for a moment. Let's say you absolutely love your rowboat. Part of your weekly routine is making sure it's impeccably clean. You keep it covered so weather doesn't damage it. The paint is flawless, and you have polished it to a near-perfect shine.

Every Sunday, for about ten minutes, you hang the boat from a tree in the yard and use it for target practice with your .22LR rifle. Meticulously, you take a single bullet and shoot it through the bottom of the boat, but you never shoot more than one bullet.

Every Monday, you bring your well-polished boat to the lake and carefully lower it into the water from your boat trailer. And every Monday you wonder why it sinks. After all the work you've done to take such good care of it six days a week, the boat still sinks every Monday.

Frustrated with the boat, you blame it for not being the boat you hoped it would be. But the situation only becomes worse because the boat keeps sinking.

Finally, you decide to talk to someone you trust about the difficulty of getting the boat to float. To your friend, Sunday's maintenance schedule seems to be the obvious obstacle to your boating desires, but you insist that your care for the boat—how you truly want the best for your boat 99.9 percent of the time—should still leave you with a fantastic boating experience on Monday. Eventually, you realize your friend is right: your boat is shipwrecked and needs to be repaired before it can operate on the water safely.

Pornography shipwrecks our marriages. The first few views might not devastate your marriage, maybe not even the first one hundred, but as the Bible puts it, "Can a man scoop fire into his lap without his clothes being burned?" (Proverbs 6:27). Pornography is a flaming heap of coals, and eventually will cause fire damage in your marriage.

The harm can manifest in subtle ways. Your spouse may feel like they are not living up to your expectations, or their self-worth may continue to decline. When pornography goes a step further, beyond viewing online, you may find yourself spiraling into live sexual experiences.

This is the reason programs like Covenant Eyes, which sends all the websites you visit to a local nun, your mom, a trusted friend, and/or your spouse, helps keep you accountable and honest. Accountability drags pornography into the light where it has a hard time thriving.

Lights. *Camera.* Action.

When we look through a camera lens, we see only what's in front of the lens. This may seem obvious, but think about your eyes as the camera lens. What you put in front of you matters. To bring a different perspective, you have to point the camera in a new direction, a new angle, or start viewing from a new distance.

KIMBERLY'S CORNER

Okay, this is for the ladies. It's not about you, but you can be part of the solution. Many women feel hurt, and their trust has been violated when they find out their husband has been looking at porn. They wonder if they aren't enough and think their husband must want someone else. These are typical, valid thoughts, but they are not the conclusion.

Our US culture is inundated with sexualized pictures of women—magazines, billboards, bumper stickers, TV shows, movies, and pornography. The truth is that men are typically more visual than women, and the marketers capitalize on that. They go after our men to get them hooked on looking at women in that way, and marketers bank on men getting so hooked that they'll pay for more of it. Those who watch porn typically don't feel great about it afterward. Like most sinful things we do, it feels good for the moment, but then the guilt and shame set in.

To be part of the solution, be kind if your husband works up the nerve to share with you that this is a problem for him. Even if you find out on your own, approach your spouse knowing that this is probably not something they are proud of. Being hurt is understandable, but you can also choose to come alongside him and work together to solve the issue. Your sin is no better than his—it just looks different.

Unraveling the past can help you determine the best angle for your camera so you experience healing in the future. When we understand how and why our struggle with pornography started, we'll have indications to the pathway for healing. Imagine for a moment that you trace your first look at pornography to your dad showing it to you and your older brothers as part of a sex talk, as he welcomed you to being a young man at age sixteen. The pathway to healing will look different than if you discovered porn while innocently typing in the wrong name on an internet search. One involves public bravado and is associated with becoming a man. One is part of a secret life no one knows about. These two introductions to porn have different paths to healing.

Remember, God is our Shepherd. He will guide you exactly the way you need to go as you listen and follow Him out of the cycle you're in. He might use a sermon, a friend, a counselor, your spouse, or some other unexpected way to give you a different perspective on the connection between your past and how that leads to healing in the present. There is no overnight fix, but recognizing what brought you to pornography puts you on the pathway to freedom.

Arguably, one of the most damaging byproducts for those who struggle with pornography is shame. Shame results when we become aware of the damage we've done by putting bullet holes through our boat. Shame prompts us to try to cover up the damage, blame others, and justify our actions as acceptable. Shame eats away at our souls.

But God gives grace to us in Jesus, and He overcame shame. Hebrews 12:2 says, "Fixing our eyes on Jesus, the pioneer and perfecter of faith. For the joy set before him he endured the cross, scorning its shame, and sat down at the right hand of the throne of God" (emphasis added). Jesus took all our sin, including shame, and nailed it to the cross. He rose victorious and invites us to live victorious with Him today. Victorious living is not some lofty ideal; it's what we experience as we walk with Jesus through every storm in life.

Shame can easily push us around and tell us that we don't deserve another chance, that we aren't enough, and that God has abandoned us to a life of addiction. Yet the hope we have in Jesus is that He will never leave us or forsake us. Shame says your marriage is doomed because of pornography, affairs, or sexual addiction, but God can lead you out of the dark past into a bright future. So, to experience healing, we give our shame to God and remind ourselves that Jesus conquered shame once and for all.

Shame thrives in darkness and isolation. We can choose to bring our story of addiction into the light, view it from a different perspective, and start a path toward healing with a plan of action. When we realize we aren't alone in our journey, we can advance toward hope and freedom.

Lights. Camera. *Action.*

Pornography usually makes its way to center stage in our marriages. If we're going to find a way out, if we're going to move toward action, we need to ask the same question Jesus asked the invalid in John 5:6: "Do you want to get well?" By the way, the man had been sick for thirty-eight years. Doesn't the answer seem obvious? But as the old saying goes, misery loves company. Sometimes we stick with what we know rather than enter into the unknown to become well, into a place where decisions must be made.

1. Whatever It Takes

If your answer to that question is, "Yes, of course I want to get well." My next question would be, "Will you do whatever it takes, no excuses?" Let me give you a couple of examples: Would you go back to a flip phone to win the battle? Would you cancel your Wi-Fi? I know. I can hear you say, "But I have work," or "I can't watch Netflix?" If you want to be well, stop making excuses and do whatever it takes to succeed. There is no comparison between surviving in marriage and having a thriving marriage—that's what you're fighting for.

2. Creating a New Story

The words we use to create our stories matter—they shape our marriages. This became clear to Kimberly and me one of the first times we left our boys at home on their own. We were enjoying a fun date when we got *the* phone call. If you're a parent, you know you have to answer that call because even though 99 percent of the time the subject matter isn't important, you never know. Usually, that call goes something like this, "Do you know where the remote for the TV is? Oh, never mind we found it." On this particular date night, however, that call was very different.

We were in the car when we got the phone call on speaker. In a panic, our middle son said, "The kitchen is on fire!" My first thought: Get off the phone and run out of there. Then our oldest ripped the phone out of his brother's hands and said, "The kitchen was on fire. We put it out."

If this were a parenting book, I'd give a thousand tips based on that one incident, but it's not. Let's say this—the words we say matter. There's a big difference between the little word *is* and its counterpart, *was*.

How we use our words to share our stories matters. Some great organizations, such as Alcoholics Anonymous, help people deal with addiction, and there are 12-step programs for pornography as well. These organization help us create new stories. Suppose you tell your spouse every day for a year, "You are an incredible child of God. You are victorious because of what God has done for you. You are an overcomer. We will get through this together. I love you no matter what." This new language, which tells a new story, would shape your marriage in awesome ways.

When we share our stories, we want to speak into who we are becoming while not cementing the story of the old life. When I talk about pornography in my marriage, I can say, "Yes, I've dealt with pornography for years, but recently I shared my struggle with my spouse, and with her help and the help of my God, I'm overcoming and experiencing hope in ways that I never have before." Kimberly and I have a better marriage now than ever before because we are learning to be real about where we've been, and we're choosing to go in a new direction together."

Speak life into each other with promises in the Bible. You can remind each other of these awesome truths:

*You are **created** in God's image.* "So God created mankind in his own image, in the image of God he created them; male and female he created them" (Genesis 1:27).

*You are **forgiven** in Christ, and I forgive you too.* "Be kind and compassionate to one another, forgiving each other, just as in Christ God forgave you" (Ephesians 4:32).

*You are **chosen** by God and I know God made you for me.* "For he chose us in him before the creation of the world to be holy and blameless in his sight" (Ephesians 1:4).

*You are **loved** unconditionally by God and me.* "And walk in the way of love, just as Christ loved us and gave himself up for us as a fragrant offering and sacrifice to God" (Ephesians 5:2).

*You are **redeemed.*** "He saved them from the hand of the foe; from the hand of the enemy he redeemed them" (Psalm 106:10).

3. Running From and Running Toward

In 2 Timothy 2:22, Paul reminds us that we not only run from the old way of life, but we also choose to run toward the new life that's filled with faith, love, and peace. "Flee the evil desires of youth and pursue righteousness, faith, love and peace, along with those who call on the Lord out of a pure heart." Today make a choice to run away from the fantasies of porn and toward the reality of creating a great marriage.

4. Knowing Your Triggers

Countless actions might trigger us to view porn. A trigger can be defined as anything that heightens your temptation. Triggers could be a place, a scent, a person, a song, a time of day, or a certain TV show or personality. Know your triggers.

Take a good look at your life, and be honest with yourself about what triggers your struggles. Talk to your spouse or a friend who can help keep you accountable—the person you trust who can help keep you on course, the person you can be open and honest with for the purpose of making your marriage the best it can be. Accountability is a huge part of your journey to success in this area.

Sharing your triggers will help others pray for you so you can experience freedom. Accountability will also remind you that keeping little secrets hinders your ability to grow closer to your spouse and to God. Sharing the real struggles going on in your life is always difficult, but the more you share them, the less hold the struggle has on you.

5. Against All Odds

God is unstoppable, and against all odds He shows us how He rescues, redeems, and changes the story of people throughout history.

> God showed up to *shut* the mouths of lions.
>
> God brought *sight* to the blind.
>
> God gives *grace* to the prostitutes.
>
> God becomes David's *strength* to slay Goliath.
>
> God *empowered* misfits of the Bible to lead.

Against all odds, God will give you His wisdom to navigate your way through pornography to an incredible marriage. Against all odds, God can redeem your marriage. Even though our marriage might be going the wrong way, God can show up in a thousand ways to show His love, His grace, and His ability to save.

CREATING MAGIC TOGETHER

TAKEAWAY

Many things can rob our marriages of true joy. Pornography is one of them. Be watchful for those things that can steal your happiness and your spouse's.

QUESTIONS

1. Ask each other: When was the last time you looked at porn?
2. What can we do to create a safe place to continue this ongoing conversation?
3. Is there anyone who can help keep us accountable in this area?

PLAN OF ACTION

At the first sign of anything that will drive a wedge between you and your spouse, discuss how that happened and what you can do to stop it. Pray together that God will open your eyes and give you wisdom to stand strong.

10

MAKING MONEY APPEAR LIKE MAGIC

Tricks to Becoming Wise with Finances

Command those who are rich in this present world not to be arrogant nor to put their hope in wealth, which is so uncertain, but to put their hope in God, who richly provides us with everything for our enjoyment.

—1 Timothy 6:17

When it comes to money, not being on the same page with your spouse will lead to arguments and frustrations. A healthy marriage involves financial wellness too.

When our marriage story started, like many other couples, we didn't have a plan for finances. We used credit cards to pay bills, hoping to gain some of the rewards that came with the cards. We paid off our bills every month for twelve years. We were winning the credit card game and racking up rewards, free travel, free hotels, free fun—until 2008 when we launched a brand-new business with one of our credit cards.

Then, with the dive of the economy, we mired ourselves in credit card debt for two years. For some of you, two years of credit card debt is nothing, but for us it was a major wake-up call. We were living week-to-week, spending every dollar. Sure, we made monthly donations to our church and gave in other ways, but we had no savings. We were focused on having fun and living in the moment.

KIMBERLY'S CORNER

Spenders vs. savers. Often one spouse is a spender and the other is a saver. We joke that Danny is the dreamer and that makes me the dream crusher. I don't recommend you use those terms unless you both are able to laugh about it.

Spending issues can create an enormous amount of tension in a marriage. This is another area where excellent communication is necessary for a happy marriage. Communicating, compromising, and holding each other accountable are all keys to winning financially and being Team Us.

Couples fight about money for many reasons, ranging from their childhood experiences with money to their buying into the need to "keep up with the Joneses." One of the best decisions we made was to use the cash/envelope system suggested by Dave Ramsey. My favorite envelope is the one labeled "Kimberly's Fun Money."

Early on in our marriage, if I spent money on clothes or something for the house, I also bought something for Danny—more out of guilt than anything else. This was a terrible plan, and when we figured out what I was doing, we made changes. But not until the fun money envelope came along did I experience true freedom in spending money. Every week a little cash gets put in each of our envelopes. We can choose to save it or spend it—so when I use my fun money, I genuinely have fun with it because it has been budgeted, and I can spend it however I want to, without guilt or any questioning.

Every time an appliance broke, a tire blew out, or something else unexpected happened, we panicked. How would we pay for it? In 2010, we decided to never use credit cards again, to save a lot, and to plan our financial future. Believe me when I say we don't have this all figured out, but here are some tricks we learned along the way.

New Mindset

Having a debt-free mindset was a new concept for us. We had assumed it was no big deal to incur some debt to enjoy nice things. I mean, who wants to drive around in a beat-up car when for a hundred dollars a month you can drive a brand-new one? If you have racked up debt, it's hard to start thinking differently about it. You've always handled finances that way, so what's the problem?

Debt is a constant weight. You may not even be aware of it until it's not there, and then you realize the joy that comes with being free of debt. Proverbs 22:7 puts it this way: "The rich rule over the poor, and the borrower is a slave to the lender." We become slaves to the bills and slaves to that way of life.

Kimberly and I made three choices regarding money, three choices I challenge you to make. Each one contributed to our ability to find freedom from the struggles money brought into our marriage.

Make a choice, as a couple, to become debt free. That's a new mindset. No excuses.

Make a choice to become generous. Having a giving mentality will transform the way you operate as a couple. Learn to look at your money as a gift from God and a blessing to be given to others, not only spent on yourselves.

Finally, make a choice to have a new mindset about money now, not later. Don't put off doing this. If you put it off until tomorrow, it could be a week, a month, or years before you put it into practice. Start now.

1. Give

I want to start with this truth: the key to making money appear like magic is to give it away. Giving frees you to trust God with your money. Many people fail to understand a key principle about giving: it is one of the greatest resources in changing the outcome of your marriage. Giving changes you, your marriage, and the world around you.

Every time you share your life, your knowledge, or your wealth with a person or a group of people, it has the potential to affect the world around you, exponentially. Giving takes guts, giving takes commitment, and ultimately, giving takes offering your best to others with no thought of recompense. Consider the following illustration.

In 2008, I decided I wanted to give big. I thought about my most valuable possessions and how I could give them away. Of all the things I owned at that time, the ones with the most value were my magic books, collected over the first twenty-five years I studied the art of illusion. Kimberly could attest to the fact that I constantly read those books. I sifted through them, practiced new ideas found in them, and at any given time, I had ten to fifteen books around my office, opened, with notebooks full of new ideas. Those books didn't just live on my shelves; they were tools to develop and create new material.

At that point in my career, I was teaching eight students around the country, from Hawaii to New York. I went to the store and bought eight large cardboard boxes, then thought about each student's expertise. I divided the books among the boxes. Some of the books were over a hundred years old, and some were selling for thousands of dollars on eBay. Each one was packaged and sent to one of my current magic students. Over the next week, phone calls and emails came in thanking me for the books. I believe this was the best thing I did in 2008.

Here's the crazy part: the students are growing in their ability to create moments of awe, and I have been more creative in the last few years than ever before. Not having the books has forced me to think magically without them—and I'm a better magician for it. The point is, you have opportunities to change the world around you by putting this principle into practice. Today. Right now. What can you give away that would help you to inspire, bless, or encourage another marriage?

2. Budgeting

To be honest, the word *budget* still makes me cringe a little. I didn't grow up budgeting, and the idea of it feels way too constraining for my free-spirited mindset. However, now that I've budgeted for years and seen the tangible benefits, I wouldn't change it for anything. A ton of books and numerous tools online can help you create a budget. *DaveRamsey.com,* which features many resources, is a great place to start. The goal of a good budget isn't to constrict you but to free you. It frees you from being a slave to bills, emergencies, and the now; it also allows you to plan, save, and create space for difficult days.

One way Kimberly and I manage finances is a weekly budget. This may seem like more work, but because my income is erratic and based on booked shows, we have times of famine and times of feasting. So, being able to plan every week was much more manageable than trying to lay out a monthly budget.

3. Automate Everything

A powerful tool for creating magic in your finances—not the disappearing type of magic but the multiplication and appearance of money—is to automate everything. Most banks and companies allow you to automatically pay your bills so you never forget to send those payments. Create accounts to automate savings—for vacations, Christmas, cars, education, emergencies, and date nights. We have many accounts that automate savings for future expenses, which put our plans into action without us thinking about it.

I don't want to oversimplify this concept of making money appear like magic, but it will. Giving to others releases money's hold on you. Budgeting assures you're spending your money wisely. And automating your saving ensures that you do it without thinking about it.

CREATING MAGIC TOGETHER

TAKEAWAY

Money can be the source of a great deal of conflict in your marriage. Most of the time these conflicts can be handled through communication, budgeting, and generosity.

QUESTIONS

1. Do you have your finances in order?
2. What would you do if you and your spouse had a million dollars (or a bigger number depending on your income)? Dream together about how you could give generously.

PLAN OF ACTION

Once you've decided the best way for you to streamline your finances, work together to make that happen. Perhaps automating some or all your bills would be a good choice. Maybe you've been married for over twenty years and have never had a budget. Now would be a good time to start. If you haven't blessed others with a financial gift in a while, maybe you both need to look at some individuals, organizations, or charities that could use some help. Give financially if you can, or give a gift of service to ministries or individuals who need some extra hands.

Create a God Pocket. Kimberly and I put cash in this envelope every week. As we go on dates or hear of other people's struggles, we look for opportunities to give away the God Pocket—which creates some great stories.

11

PLAYING THE CARDS YOU'RE DEALT

Learning to Deal with Life's Challenges

I have told you these things, so that in me you may have peace. In this world you will have trouble. But take heart! I have overcome the world.

—John 16:33

Gambling effects with blackjack and poker (basically cheating with cards) fascinate me. With my skill set, I could easily take advantage of others. Cheating is rather easy with thirty years of experience handling a deck of cards. Yet all my knowledge is used for entertainment purposes—until now. I want to teach you how to cheat, not with cards but with your spouse.

As a magician, if I'm dealt a lousy hand, I have dozens of methods for changing it into a great hand. Cheating at cards usually involves small, simple manipulations that alter the outcome of the game for the cheater. Cheating at cards has the potential to shorten your life but cheating to improve your marriage can flip the script regardless of the hand you've been dealt.

Some people are dealt mental health issues. Some marriage partners have had a disproportionate amount of sadness, loss, and pain. Some deal with difficult trust issues. Yet, regardless of the hand we're dealt, we can learn to thrive through life's challenges. Here are some ways to experience the best marriage possible.

Small Things Matter

A pin-sized dot on a playing card, known as a marked deck, is a small change that can tell me whether another player is holding a pair of aces or a hand of unplayable cards. Small things matter. The key for experiencing joy in any circumstance is to consistently make small changes in the right direction.

Let's say you want to change the way you think about yourself. Put a sticky note on your mirror that says, "But to all who did receive Him, who believed in His name, He gave the right to become children of God" (John 1:12 ESV). Read it daily. This might take you less than a minute, but it reminds you every day that you're a son or daughter of the King. It assures you that God sees you, He cares for you, and you are not alone. Maybe you read the verse a thousand times before its truth sinks in—you are loved and you're His. But the small decision to write down a verse and read it daily changes the outcome of your thinking.

"Who dares make light of small beginnings" (Zechariah 4:10 NET)? Nobody. Small is the way change starts—from building a skyscraper to growing an apple tree, or to creating a thriving marriage. "Whoever can be trusted with very little can also be trusted with much, and whoever is dishonest with very little will also be dishonest with much" (Luke 16:10).

Actions, Faith and Decisions

Oscar Wilde said, "One should always play fairly when one has the winning cards."[8] I was invited to a friendly poker game with the specific purpose of cheating. This involved a group of four guys who met in college, and once a year for the last twenty years they got together to play poker for the night. Yes, they played for money, but for nineteen years everything was always friendly—until I showed up.

We'll call my friend who brought me into the game Roger. He said to me, "When I give you the nod, you deal everyone a great hand, but make sure I come out the winner!" He also said that he'd keep track of the money and make sure everything went back to the original players after the hand was played.

The house was filled with chips, sodas, appetizers, and a poker table. I was introduced and asked if I could play. The other guys were happy to take this new sucker's money. So we played and played. Probably for three or four hours. In this friendly game, everyone got a chance to be the dealer. We rotated after each game. When the deck was handed to me, Roger gave me the nod.

I'll spare you the exact hands that I dealt to each player, but let's just say that everyone had an exceptional hand. I've never heard so much trash talk. Everyone took on a new air of cockiness. Language was exchanged. Roger held his hand and smiled, knowing he had the winning hand. The bets grew bigger and bigger. If this had been a game of Texas Hold 'Em, everyone would have been all in. But there was no maximum, so everyone kept getting their wallets out. One guy took out his credit card to make his bet and said, "I'm good for it." All the trash talk faded to complete silence as the moment of truth came.

When the first person threw his cards face up on table, it seemed like an unbeatable hand—until the next person threw an even better hand, then the next, then the next. Then they all looked at Roger. He turned over a royal flush, the highest hand in poker. As Roger went to grab all the money on the table, he broke the news: "Alright, guys, my friend is a professional magician. I told him to cheat."

They weren't interested in any magic. They were mad to say the least. In fact, that poker game has continued for the last ten years, and every time an email goes out for the invite and the location, it starts with "Hi Everyone, no magicians allowed! Is that clear?" Needless to say, I was never invited back.

But imagine for a moment that you had the ability to cheat like that in your marriage. What if you could always have a winning hand? What if God wants to deal you the winning hand?

You can cheat the system by giving your hand (your life and marriage) to God daily. What might seem like a lousy hand can quickly turn into a winning hand, especially if you give everything to God. You see, our actions are born out of decisions. Great marriages don't magically happen; they are created. Regardless of the hand you're dealt, you can use what you have to create magic together.

Creating an amazing marriage isn't a passive challenge about waiting to see what happens. It's a callout to God to say, "Would You deal me a better hand this next season, or will You change this hand into a winning hand? Would you show us how to win with the hand we currently have? But no matter what happens, we'll give everything we have to You!" Marriage requires that you never stop giving your best to your spouse. This action involves your complete and total participation. Decide to do something about your marriage today.

Pray Together

Something massive in your marriage takes place when you pray with your spouse. Prayer is essentially saying, "God, would You deal in our favor today?" Praying together is intimate. Praying together is deep. Praying together is the single most transformative action you can take in your marriage. When you pray together, it's like showing up to a game of poker with the world's best card cheat. It positions you to understand that with God on your side, He will find a way for you to win.

Create a Clarity of Desire

I've been actively studying the art of magic for over thirty years. It's a fascinating subject that continues to challenge different areas of my life. The best tricks in history all have one thing in common—clarity of effect.

> "The Statue of Liberty disappeared!"
>
> "My signed quarter appeared in a lime!"
>
> "My wife was sawn in two!"
>
> "He dealt me a royal flush—seven times!"

The worst effects lack clarity. "I took a card. He placed seven cards, no wait ... it was ten cards on the table. ... I really don't know what happened next, but he found my card." Tricks that lack clarity of effect lack power. One of the most powerful tools for creating a better marriage is knowing what you (as a couple) want and how you are going to get there.

Let me give you an example of a marriage that lacks clarity.

The wife says, "I might as well not even be in the room. It's like I'm invisible to him. He's way more interested in sports on TV or his phone, and even his work is more important than me. I've tried talking to him, but he doesn't listen, and I don't think he even cares. He never notices how I look. My friend at work sure notices when I look good. Sometimes it feels like this relationship has run its course, and it would be better to just start over with someone else."

The husband says, "She doesn't listen. She's always depressed. She never does what I want. She says, 'If you'd just read this book, you'd understand me.' She knows I'm not reading some dumb book. I told her if she wants a better marriage then she could start putting out more. I'm sick of her, and this marriage is over if I don't fix what she has broken."

The pain of these statements makes it clear that this marriage is in deep trouble if the couple doesn't make significant changes soon. If your marriage reflects this scenario in the slightest, I encourage you to

KIMBERLY'S CORNER

Sometimes our marriage isn't going well, or we are stuck in unhealthy patterns and need help. There's nothing wrong with that; in fact, it's wise to recognize you need help and have the courage to seek it.

Finding a good counselor to help you with communication and the issues you face within your marriage can be life changing. A professional can give you tools to put in your toolbox so you can learn to make healthy changes in your relationship.

Some people place stigmas on counseling, but I don't understand that mindset. I'm so thankful my mother always said, "You go to a doctor when your body needs fixing, so it only makes sense to go to a professional when your mind or heart is hurting." I also love that when my brother and I were kids, Mom often said, "I'm doing the best I can, and I will pay for your therapy!" And the truth is, she did an amazing job, but she has also paid for my therapy at times.

become very clear about what you want and how you're going to get there. Remember Roger in the story above. He knew exactly what he wanted (to win the game) and how he was going to get there—bring a wizard (card wizard at least). Making choices together to make changes will create magic in your marriage.

For example, "We're having a difficult time listening and hearing each other, but we've decided to do whatever it takes to create a thriving marriage. Starting today, we won't use never and always statements like 'You're never on time' or 'You always forget my birthday.' Starting today, we'll listen to an audible book on effective communication. Starting today, we'll plan on dating once a week. Starting today, we'll pray together."

The key to making change is to clarify what you and your spouse want from the marriage. Maybe ask your spouse, "What's one change you would like me to make to help us create a better marriage?"

By becoming clear on what you want and how you're going to do it, you'll significantly increase your ability to create a great marriage together.

Learn to Enjoy Each Other

It sounds obvious that you and your spouse should enjoy each other, but so many marriages are struggling because the closer a person becomes to their spouse, the more flaws they see. Seeing these flaws, they enjoy (not love) their spouse less. The imperfections of our spouse aren't meant to keep us from each other but to help us to love each other the way God loves us. God doesn't love you because you are flawless; He chooses to love you in spite of your imperfections.

The people in your life who love you the most put up with your idiosyncrasies and weirdness. They simply love you, for you. Learning to love your spouse and enjoy all their God-given oddness will bring both of you joy.

Becoming Invisible

I love watching young magicians do everything fast. It reminds me of when I was a teenager and thought good magic was about speed. I worked on certain sleights so I could do them superfast. What I started to hear was "Man, you are fast with your hands. I thought I saw something, but wow, you are quick!" What I learned was that moving fast creates horrible magic. Sure, speed generates lots of compliments, but the goal isn't doing something superfast but doing it so fast and flawless that the sleight is invisible. Had I shown up at the poker game and created suspicion by doing everything fast, the other players would have been a lot more cautious with their bets.

When something is invisible, people don't say, "Wow. That's crazy how fast you did that." Instead, they say nothing about *how* I did it; they simply say, "That's impossible. I have no idea how you did that!" Creating mind-blowing effects is my goal, and that happens by making moves invisible, not making them fast.

In making our marriages great, it's not the speed at which we make change that matters most. Rather, we need to focus on the small, imperceptible changes over time that create the impossible changes we need. Take, for instance, the spouse who goes to a marriage conference or reads a book about ninety-nine ways to build a great marriage. When he comes home, he says, "We're going implement these ninety-nine principles on Monday, so we can have a great marriage by the end of the week." Obviously, that's an exaggeration, but most of us want change, and we want it now.

Invisible changes are more like a small rudder on a ship that makes minute adjustments to redirect the ship in a new direction. We don't need instantaneous changes that last for a day, a month, or a year. No, we need invisible, almost unnoticeable changes that alter the course of our lives.

When I was twenty-three years old, someone told me that Jesus never spoke one negative word about Himself. After hearing that, I made a silent, invisible promise to not say negative things about myself. I've broken that promise many times, but as a rule, I don't say, "I'm an idiot!" or "Why am I so dumb?" Most people don't notice that habit, but it's an invisible change that has significantly altered the direction of my life.

Small changes, invisible changes, alter the trajectory of your marriage.

Of course, playing the hand you're dealt is far more difficult than making a few changes. But as we become more and more aware of our flaws, our struggles, and our advantages, we'll position ourselves to create the best marriage possible given our unique situation. Thankfully, Jesus told us that "in this world you will have trouble. But take heart! I have overcome the world" (John 16:33). He didn't promise that everything on earth would be perfect, including our marriage. He promised to be with us through everything. So take heart. Jesus is with you, and He will help you overcome the problems you face today, tomorrow, and every day of your life.

CREATING MAGIC TOGETHER

TAKEAWAY

Hardship is unavoidable, but James chapter one reminds us of how we can grow through the difficult seasons of life and marriage. Challenges can bring us closer to God and to each other.

QUESTIONS

Put a verse somewhere you will read it every day. What verse do you need to read daily? Why? Discuss this with your spouse. What verse would your spouse choose? If you don't know, talk through your greatest spiritual needs and help each other find the right verse.

PLAN OF ACTION

Think about why you fell in love with your spouse. Write down some attributes that helped you fall in love with them. Then write down some things you love about your spouse right now. Keep this list close to you. Tell your spouse at least one of the things you love about them. From this day on, pick one thing each day to tell your spouse that you love about them. Surprise them with a note on the bathroom mirror, in a purse or briefcase, or on the steering wheel of the car.

12

PICK A CARD, ANY CARD

Choosing to Run Your Race with Joy

He is before all things, and in him all things hold together.

—Colossians 1:17

When people talk about how difficult marriage is, they sometimes say, "If we were meant to be together, why is it so hard?" or "Shouldn't love be easier?" or "I'm not sure this is worth the work to fix."

What if I decided that creating great magic is too hard? What if I said, "It's not worth the practice it takes to create a one-of-a-kind magical experience"?

What if Tiger Woods had given up on golf because his ball landed in too many sand traps during a tournament?

What if Michelangelo had decided that painting the ceiling of the Sistine Chapel upside down was too hard?

Imagine a world without magic. A world without spectacular athletes. A world where masterpieces like the ceiling of the Sistine Chapel don't exist.

In chapter 11 we talked about creating a clarity of desire, dealing with life's challenges, and making the small invisible changes that lead to a better marriage. Those ideas sound great, until you start working on them. Change is hard, but we choose to engage and to press through the difficult times to experience joy and fulfillment. We work hard because a great marriage is magical, full of highlights, and incredibly fulfilling.

Our marriages are under constant attack, stress, and scrutiny. As couples, we must learn to endure. Endure suffering. Endure being misunderstood. Endure loss. Endure when you feel distant from or not in love with your spouse. Marriage is a marathon through uncharted territory, not a sprint on a comfortable track. In Hebrews 12:1–2, the author reminds us to endure:

Therefore, since we are surrounded by so great a cloud of witnesses, let us also lay aside every weight, and sin which clings so closely, and let us run with endurance the race that is set before us, looking to Jesus, the founder and perfecter of our faith, who for the joy that was set before him endured the cross, despising the shame, and is seated at the right hand of the throne of God (ESV, emphasis added).

The author of Hebrews uses the Greek word *hypomone* (translated "endurance"), which means "a person who is not swerved from his deliberate purpose and his loyalty to faith and piety by even the greatest trials and sufferings."[9] I find this word fascinating in the context of our marriages. What would our marriages look like if we were deliberate in achieving the promises of marriage: to have and to hold; for richer, for poorer; in sickness and in health; to love and to cherish 'til death do us part? What if we remained loyal despite the greatest trials and sufferings? What if we always chose to endure?

Learning to Run

These verses unlock the secrets to enduring the most difficult times. First, we remember that we are not alone. If you've run in a special event (a 5k charity run, a marathon, etc.), the part that makes these races fun, despite the physical challenges, is that you are running with other people. From the moment you leave the starting line until the thrilling moment where you finish, you are with others. In fact, often, teams run or walk the entire course together!

In the same way, we can take encouragement from the fact that other couples are already running a good marriage race, and we can learn much from them. You are not alone!

Most people treat their spouse differently in public. They are less likely to raise their voice or say something that would shame their spouse publicly. Knowing that we are never really on our own reminds us to respect, cherish, and love our spouse regardless of where we are.

Second, look closely at the next part of the passage because the point is easy to miss: "lay aside every weight and sin which clings so closely." I'm not a huge fan of those tiny running shorts that marathoners like to wear, but when you're trying to complete a long run, you don't want to carry any extra weight or hinderances. It's not often that you see a distance runner in blue jeans and cowboy boots.

It's easy to say, "Well, I'm not doing anything wrong, so I'm not going to make any changes." Sometimes what's best for your marriage isn't a matter of right and wrong, but a matter of good and great, or better and best.

Obviously, there are behaviors which are clearly wrong (beating your spouse, lying to your spouse, gossiping about your spouse), but there are also weights that can slow us down. Again, these aren't necessarily sins, but they make running a good marriage race nearly impossible.

KIMBERLY'S CORNER

Danny writes, "Where we look changes our perspective," and that is no joke. To know me, is to know that I do not like to exercise (yes I know I should). However, on the rare occasion that I have physically pushed myself, people ask, "Now, didn't that feel great? Aren't you glad you did it?!" And my answer thus far, is "no, I don't feel great, but I guess I am proud of myself for doing it."

(Continued)

These bouts of pathetic excuses for athleticism are few and far between. I typically only say yes to Danny's crazy adventure ideas (like hiking a hill to see a sunrise) when we are on vacation. Since this has been a pattern for so long, Danny has decided that my alter-ego who says yes to exercise is "Vacation Kimberly." I am totally okay with that and think it's kind of funny. In fact lately, I have made it a point to try to say more yeses and be more like Vacation Kimberly even when we are not traveling.

The most recent "yes" was to a hike in the hills near our house. We brought the two dogs and it started out well... until it got steeper and harder. Naturally, I am out of shape, so it didn't not take long for my lungs to start burning and I was no longer responding to Danny as he talked (who was not even slightly winded)! He was very patient with me and he is always a great encourager.

I took breaks while he ran the dogs, and then they came return to walk with me again. I had a lot of time to think on that hill, and a lot of times where I wanted to turn back and go home. I took a moment to turn around to see where I had been and enjoy the view, and other moments I looked up at the "mountain" in front of me and told Danny I was headed home or just going to die right there. But then I remembered how it must be for so many people who are struggling in life right now. Maybe some of you are stuck looking at the past, instead of realizing it is good that you are no longer there. Maybe others of you are looking at the life ahead of you, wanting to quit just like I wanted to quit the hike.

When I finally decided to just take one step at a time and just keep moving forward little by little, I was surprised when I made it to our goal. My lungs were still burning, but I was proud of myself for reaching my goal. I probably won't say yes to that hike again any time soon, but I am glad I did it because it gave me a different perspective, and that "yes" helped me to realize sometimes it's just about putting one foot in front of the other.

What could a simple "yes" do for your marriage?

There are weights of work, weights of household responsibilities, some crazy family members (everybody has at least one), kids' schedules, deadlines, bills, vacations, work trips, and side hustles. None of these are inherently wrong, but they can become extra weights that hinder your marriage and prevent you and your spouse from experiencing grace, joy, and celebration.

Third, to run this race of endurance, we need to acknowledge that God has put it "before us." When you participate in a running event, you know that the course was designed and laid out intentionally. Sometimes you might think the course designer wasn't as thoughtful as they could have been, or maybe you love every turn, switchback, and straightaway. Either way, you know that the course was set out purposefully to achieve a certain objective.

In our marriages, we often feel trapped when looking back and wondering what could or would have happened if we had turned left instead of right, if we had not taken the promotion, or not purchased the bigger house. Instead, don't focus on what's behind you, but focus on the path in front of you. The past doesn't have to define who you are. The past might say, "You'll never become anything. You were always like this. You can't do it. Look at your history. Look at your family. You can't!" But you can speak truth and hope into your present and future, and choose to redeem a difficult past.

Today we declare that God has designed a race that's marked out specifically for each of us and for each of our marriages. Today we declare that we're going to live according to our God-given purpose and step into God's plan for our marriage. Today we are going to endure the trials and suffering and say yes to everything that God wants for us.

Finally, to run a good race you have to know where to look. Where we look changes our perspective on everything. If I'm looking behind me, it's going to be hard to know what's ahead of me. I have never seen a runner win a race while looking over their shoulder the entire time. But I have seen runners miss turns, take a spill on the pavement, or even lead others down the wrong road when they weren't paying attention. When we don't fix our eyes in the right place, we have the potential of running way off course.

So, the author of Hebrews tells us to look to Jesus and follow His example. Do what He did. He endured the cross and did it with joy because He knew the outcome would be the saving of many lives. We can look online, to friends, to teachers, to books, and to anything and anyone for answers. Or we can look to Jesus. We can trust that He is an extraordinary teacher, shepherd, and God and that He will lead us according to His plan.

Choosing Joy

The journey to change can be hard, but it can be filled with happiness and joy. Happiness can be discovered in the best of times; joy can be experienced in the worst of times. Joy springs, not from circumstances, but from the vision of creating magic together in your marriage. You can endure almost anything if you can picture a better future—Team Us forever.

So, what do we do when things become difficult?

I was riding my bike up a steep incline recently—a 1,243-foot climb over a short distance on a single-speed bike. On the last part of the climb, I was panting, sweating, and ready to quit. Then I saw a message spray-painted on the asphalt: "It's just a hill. Enjoy." The words made me laugh, but they also helped me to stay focused and to push through the pain.

Every marriage will have pressures, stresses, and unforeseen circumstances that feel like an uphill battle. Whether it's finances, or health, workplace tension, or something else altogether—whatever you're going through today—remember, it's just a hill. Enjoy.

Okay, you say, it's just a hill, but uphill climbs are tough. And seriously, is it really possible to enjoy the climb? When we receive bad news from a doctor, an anniversary is forgotten again, or our spouse is short-tempered because of a book deadline—oh wait, that's just me!—uphill climbs are difficult. These moments are never easy on a marriage. Yet in these moments, we can discover our true character. In these moments, we learn to press through adversity, together. We push through, together. We never give up. We give it our all. We pray. We sweat. We live with purpose. And uphill climbs are opportunities for us to experience joy at all times. But how?

1. Perspective. Try to see your problems and struggles from a different perspective. No matter how difficult your marriage is today, you're still together. Finding joy today means you'll have to see the situation from a different angle. Gaining perspective on your uphill climb gives you the ability to have joy in the midst of pain.

When Kimberly and I were in the Neonatal Care Unit with two of our children, we were devastated, and it was difficult to find joy. God reminded us that we could pray for the other babies, love and encourage the other moms and dads, and be thankful for every moment we could spend with our kids. The understanding that other people were in a similar situation—some with worse medical conditions—combined with the heart God gave us to pray for them helped shift our perspective and find joy in our pain.

2. Thankfulness. Pain is often a reminder of how much has been good in our marriages, yet we weren't thankful for those times. Uphill climbs remind us to be thankful despite our circumstances, and thankfulness leads us back to joy.

When you're in a lot of pain, you often find it's easier to empathize with others. Pain gives you a unique opportunity to connect with others in pain. Giving thanks in these circumstances is difficult, but it shapes us to bless and encourage others in hard times.

Kimberly occasionally experiences debilitating migraines. Sometimes they build slowly throughout the day, and sometimes they come on suddenly, but the results are the same. She is a strong woman, so when she goes down with one of these migraines, I know she is experiencing severe pain. But her migraines have given her even greater compassion and empathy for others in pain. Empathy is key to her being compassionate in the office, and even though her migraines are terrible, she's thankful for how God uses them to influence her work.

3. Choice. Joy is a choice. Joy is an understanding that there is hope for our marriage. In the midst of pain, choosing to trust that God knows how to help us is choosing to find joy in our trials.

Choosing joy happens as you see the situation from a different perspective. You are thankful regardless of the circumstances, so you build your ability to enjoy the moment even when others would choose to complain.

My good friend Joe preached at our church a few years ago. During his message, he talked about a season of life with his wife, Traci, and their three kids, after he was let go from a ministry position. The loss of that job included the loss of his housing, at a time when they were living far from any family. The change was sudden and unexpected; Joe and Traci found themselves literally homeless and jobless virtually overnight.

In his message, Joe shared a key thought that helped him and Traci navigate that season with joy and thankfulness. They made three choices the first night after being let go. They chose to believe that God was not surprised by their circumstances. They chose to start and end each day by acknowledging three things for which they were thankful, and they journaled about them together. Finally, they chose to keep following God, even though the next eight months were some of the hardest of their married lives.

Today, Joe and Traci would tell you how important those choices were. Their marriage stayed strong during that season, they grew more connected to each other and to God, and they found reasons to be joyful and thankful every day. That joy and thankfulness were the result of their choices.

Remember, it's just a hill. Enjoy.

Perspective, thankfulness, and choice lead us to a radically transformed marriage as we find joy in midst of the ups and downs of life. We all have excuses as to why life is too difficult for us to be joyful. But Paul challenges us to our core when he writes, "I am greatly encouraged; in all our troubles my joy knows no bounds" (2 Corinthians 7:4). Not in some of our troubles, but in all our troubles joy can be discovered in huge quantities no matter what the condition our marriage is.

CREATING MAGIC TOGETHER

TAKEAWAY

Talk about 1 Thessalonians 5:16–18. How can you choose joy?

How can you be thankful in difficult times? Talk about some of the hard times you've been through as a couple. Ask God to keep you mindful of choosing joy over anything else.

QUESTIONS

Recall a time when you didn't choose joy. What were the consequences? How would a different choice have made a difference?

PLAN OF ACTION

Reflect with your spouse about a hard time. Was there some joy in it? Was there change because of the hardship? Could you have done something or reacted differently to have made the journey easier? What did you learn from that experience?

SECTION 3

SECRETS TO THRIVING IN MARRIAGE

This section is the climax of all the secrets I'm giving you. This is the section we want to build toward in our marriage after we have developed good or great communication skills—communication that leads toward intimacy and results. When by God's grace we are overcoming the impossible obstacles that stand between us and a thriving marriage, then we can begin to create and expect our marriages to thrive.

I want to challenge you to take your marriage to the next level of intimacy. The next level of giving. The next level of grace and forgiveness so you can experience over-the-top moments and focus on Team Us forever!

This section is the driving force of the entire book—what we want our marriages to be. A thriving marriage takes two people who consistently do whatever it takes to create a great marriage.

Christmas Eve 1999, Kimberly and I are about to leave for San Diego. Our newborn is secured in his baby carrier. We are about to walk out the door, when she says, "The Christmas tree is crooked."

I look at it and say to myself, "Okay, that's nice. Let's go."

She stands back and says, "Can you fix it?"

At that time in my life, I had a fixation with being on time, and ideally, arriving early. In my mind, we had about two minutes to rush out the door. But to oblige my wife, I crawl under the tree and grab hold of the sappy tree with my left hand to try to straighten it out; with the other hand, I screw the wing-nut bolt into the base of the tree.

She says, "That's perfect."

I back out from under pine-tree needles that are poking me in the back of my neck. As soon as I stand up, the tree starts to lean again.

She says, "Um, honey?"

"Yep, I see it." I scrabble back under the tree again. This happens multiple times. I get out from under the tree, and ten seconds later, the tree starts to lean. To say that I'm frustrated is an understatement. We should have left fifteen minutes ago. Who cares about a stupid crooked tree right now? She does!

I am back under the tree, and my lovely wife says things like, "Maybe just try screwing in a different spot," and "Can you push the bolts in harder?"

Finally, the tree is in place. She smiles. "You did it. Thank you."

And then the tree leans again.

Keep in mind the tree is adorned with our favorite childhood ornaments. I grab the tree with both hands, lift it up, and slam it onto the floor. Over and over again. Ornaments fly through the air and crash to pieces on the floor.

After doing this several times, the tree is finally straight.

Not even five seconds later, it leans again.

Kimberly doesn't say a word. She sees how ridiculously angry I am.

I grab my keys, walk out the door, jump in the car, and drive to the nearest Ace hardware store. I find a Christmas tree stand. The label says, "Simply pump the foot pedal. Set up your Christmas tree in less than a minute! No assembly required, no screws to tighten!" I didn't check the price. I didn't care. I say to myself, "I will set my stopwatch, and if this tree is not up in one minute, I'm returning it."

I go home and rip the box open like the Hulk. Didn't read any instructions. Set my stopwatch, and forty-eight seconds later, we have a tree standing perfectly straight. "Let's go, babe."

The ride to San Diego was ice cold because I failed big time with my attitude, my anger, and my choice to handle the situation the way I did.

But I learned two things. One, if I'm going to create a thriving marriage, I can't act like that. Second, the right tools matter. That tree stand was serious magic. If I had purchased it earlier, it would have saved me a lot of embarrassment and foolish behavior. Sometimes having the right tools will enable you to solve problems quickly and effectively. Yet all the right tools will mean nothing if you don't use them properly.

13

PRACTICE. PRACTICE. PRACTICE

Creating Better Habits

Therefore everyone who hears these words of mine and puts them into practice is like a wise man who built his house on the rock.

—Matthew 7:24

Magicians practice for countless hours to do an invisible move that takes less than a second. These secret moves allow them to create seemingly impossible moments. Yet if a magician practices the move incorrectly, all the practice time in the world won't make it perfect. In our marriages, we have to invest countless hours in the right ways to care for our spouse if we want to experience a better marriage and relationship. The book of Isaiah reminds us to "stop doing wrong. Learn to do right" (1:16–17).

This chapter takes a hard look at the struggles, habits, and sins that have taken root in our marriages. I challenge you to stop doing the things that are hurting and hindering you from creating a better marriage, and I encourage you to start practicing grace, forgiveness, thankfulness, joy, and prayer.

Creating Better Habits

Before a first date, it's always a bad idea when a friend says, "I dare you to ..." Trust me, anything that follows that statement can't be good, but that is exactly where I found myself before a first date my freshman year of college. My friend Travis said, "On your date, I dare you to give her a blow nose." For those not familiar with a blow nose, let me explain: to execute the perfect blow nose, you place your mouth over someone else's nose and then blow as hard as you can. If done properly, the other person involuntarily makes a honking noise that sounds something like a pigeon being squeezed by a five-year-old. Of course, not having much of a social filter at nineteen years of age, I accepted Travis's dare.

So there we were, my future wife and I, out on our first date. We went on a hike to Forest Falls in southern California to enjoy a waterfall, a picnic, and some great laughs. Then, at the right moment, I leaned in. Kimberly thought I was leaning in for a kiss, but I placed my mouth over her nose and *hoooooooonk!* She was in complete shock.

She then let me know that if I ever did that again, the relationship would be over. Despite that bad first-date decision, she agreed to a second date, and thankfully, she is still with me.

That wasn't the last time I listened to dumb advice. However, I learned to break that habit and not surprise Kimberly with a dumb juvenile bet. I want to help you to avoid making some dumb decisions and empower you to unlock the incredible marriage that God has designed for you.

Every marriage will be full of mistakes—it's what you do with those mistakes that matters. You can choose to grow from them, or you can choose to let those mistakes shape your life and relationship. Mistakes aren't meant to define you. Mistakes may deter you. They may draw you offtrack, but only God gets to speak His plan, His purpose, His story into our lives—God as Creator gets to remind you of the purposes for which He has created you by His grace and love. Our job is to focus our minds on God's plan for our marriage. In doing that, you'll be able to put into practice His plans for you and your spouse.

Doing the same old things over and over again will continue to fail. Now's the time to start putting new and better habits into practice.

We need to consistently practice the right way to create magic in our marriage. Let's start with a few habits that can change the trajectory of your marriage.

Thankfulness

Say thank you more often. Showing your spouse your deep appreciation creates a new mindset for your marriage. "Thank you for working so hard." "Thank you for cleaning up." "Thank you for taking time to listen." "Thank you for going to bed with me." "Thank you for making the bed." Expressing our thanks often positions us to experience more joy in our marriages.

12-Hour Prayer Journey (12HPJ)

Another habit that will transform your marriage is the 12-Hour Prayer Journey. Before I tell you more about 12HPJ, don't you think that if, as a couple, you prayed for twelve hours, it could have a positive impact on your marriage? Think about it. Twelve hours of asking the King of the Universe to help you, to guide you, and to transform your marriage. If you receive nothing else out of this book and you implement this one practice, in two years I believe you will have a completely different marriage.

Pray together for twelve hours. Okay, that seems like a lot, right? But that twelve hours is broken up over a year by praying one minute in the morning together and one minute at night. Two minutes times 365 equals 760 minute. Now divide that by sixty minutes in an hour, and you get 12.66. In other words, two minutes of prayer a day adds up to twelve plus hours of prayer in a year.

KIMBERLY'S CORNER

"What's the magic word?"

Our American culture tends to make a big deal out of teaching children to say please and thank you. But why do so many adults think it's okay to drop the practice when they're older, or worse, they say it to a friend or coworker but not to their husband or wife?

In our house, a couple chores are somewhat assigned, but basically chores are a team effort all the time. If I see the garbage piling up, I'm not helpless. I can take it out, but sometimes life is super busy, and I choose to walk by it as it is overflowing. I might ask Danny if he has a minute to do it, but often, I don't have to ask because he just does it. If I had to guess why he chooses to do it, I'd say that it's because he knows I appreciate it. Because my love language is acts of service, I'm genuinely grateful, so I tell him, "Thank you."

We try not to take each other for granted, and a powerful way of doing that is to respectfully tell each other, "Thank you."

This habit ensures that you start and end the day on the same page, which is crucial for creating a thriving marriage. The incremental positive changes you make today significantly change the future of your marriage.

Getting Rid of Old Habits

I had the opportunity to perform on Penn & Teller's TV show, *Fool Us*—a program designed to see if magicians can fool the most knowledgeable magicians in the business. When they sent me the confirmation email that said, "See you in Vegas!" I thought my work was done. No, no, no! I met with their executive team for three months, doing grueling work day and night, fixing old habits that I wasn't even aware were affecting my performance.

The piece I performed is called Eyeball Roulette, a trick where I play a game of Russian roulette with my eyeball. I know, not my brightest idea. They watched the routine thirty-one times over ninety days and gave me hundreds of corrections to make it ready for prime time. The corrections were difficult because, after doing the illusion a thousand times, I thought it was nearly perfect. Penn and Teller's team made the effect even better by taking out the old habits that hindered the illusion.

Breaking old habits in our marriages is hard but worth the work. To start breaking the habits that are holding you back from a better marriage, be transparent with your spouse about habits that are hurting you, them, or the marriage as a whole. This conversation may be painful, but it can also bring a lot of hope in the days to come. Follow the principles from section one on communication to ensure you have a healthy conversation that moves you forward to break old habits.

Let's say, in that conversation your spouse says, "I wouldn't normally share this but because you are asking for help breaking habits that hurt or hinder our marriage, I want you to know it hurts me that you complain about the way I look. When you say, 'I wouldn't wear that,' it hurts. It seems small to you, but it hurts because I hear 'I don't like the way you look.' I know you're only talking about the clothes, but that's not how I hear it."

You respond by saying, "I completely understand. I'll work on breaking that habit."

Now that you are aware of this old habit, you want to make a plan with your spouse to create a new habit to replace the old one.

If your spouse has asked you to address areas that need change in their life, you can help your spouse and be a major part of the solution. Instead of nagging or showing disappointment, you can encourage, support, and show grace as your spouse works to create new habits. Being part of the change is essential to letting your spouse know you want to share the struggles and pain of transformation.

Be Honest

I was out to eat with my family recently when I noticed an older couple a few tables over, talking and laughing together. They were probably in their mid-eighties, but they looked good. I leaned over to Kimberly and said, "That's going to be us some day." I spoke too soon because I definitely didn't anticipate what came next.

The wife politely excused herself to use the restroom. The husband waited until she was out of sight, then he reached over to the next table, grabbed a handful of creamers, opened them, and chugged them like he was doing shots of tequila. He must have downed nine or ten creamers before he shoved the containers in his pocket and waited patiently for his wife to return.

Clearly, he didn't want his wife knowing about his creamer addiction. I'm sure that would be a tough habit to break. I'm sure his wife knew he loved creamer, but she was probably living under the assumption that he was free from his old life of slamming creamers at a restaurant. To move forward in creating better habits, we have to be honest with our spouse and give our spouse the opportunity to be a part of the solution. If we nag or show disappointment, we'll encourage a secret life of creamer shots.

Practice

Making changes in a relationship is hard work, and like most changes in life, require practice. If you had the privilege of watching Mozart practice the piano, you wouldn't expect perfection. If Mozart was doing a dress rehearsal, you wouldn't expect a flawless concert. Expectations change our attitudes.

What would happen if, as a couple, you agreed to help each other practice new habits? In this process, you give room for failures, mistakes, and slipping back into old habits. But you also give space for healthy correction and encouragement to keep going. Pressing on in this practice environment will be far more productive and effective than if after one mistake you say, "I knew you'd never change." Allowing room for growth and change takes time and practice.

Changing your mindset and implementing new strategies for growth in your marriage will create a better relationship. Remember to show grace and forgiveness. Remind your spouse that you are on their team and that you are for them. Inspire them to become the person they are designed to be as they inspire you to become who you are designed to be. You are a team. Team Us forever!

CREATING MAGIC TOGETHER

TAKEAWAY

Kindness and consideration toward your spouse can become a habit if you practice it regularly. Learning to really listen to our spouse can help us better understand what words and actions build them up and can help you grow better habits.

QUESTIONS

1. Ask your spouse: What's one habit you need to break?
2. Ask your spouse: What's one habit you need to start?
3. Ask your spouse: Are you also willing to drop a habit and add one?
4. Create a plan together to implement new habits and eliminate old habits. Be gracious.

PLAN OF ACTION

On your date night this week, take along a blank piece of paper for each of you. Without any discussion, write down what your spouse does that makes you feel cared for. Then include a few actions that aren't on the list but would make you feel the same way. Discuss the list and how you can help your spouse create new habits that show love and respect for each other.

Carefully and kindly talk with your spouse about a habit you would like them to break. (Start with a small one.) Also ask them to share one habit that you need to break. Make a plan for working on it, having in mind that it will take time, grace, and effort. Meet back together in a week to see what progress you've made and to give and receive feedback.

14

BACKSTAGE

Growing in Intimacy with God

Arise, cry out in the night, as the watches of the night begin; pour out your heart like water in the presence of the Lord.

— Lamentations 2:19

Nothing is quite like close-up magic. A great close-up routine creates intimacy and builds a deep connection with participants because of the childlike experience. In a day and age when we have lost our sense of wonder and amazement, close-up magic reminds us that deeper mysteries exist in the world; it touches us emotionally.

There is a direct correlation, a mysterious connection between your intimacy with God and your intimacy with your spouse. Intimacy with God is the driving force of being satisfied in this life. Everything is contingent on our relationship with God. We will have ups and downs, but the Creator of the universe is unchanging. We are in constant motion, and God moves with us to reveal His love, His passion, His power, and His life. Intimacy with God changes everything.

Your perspective.

Your direction.

Your purpose.

Your relationships.

Your attitude.

Your marriage.

Intimacy with God is a hard concept to express. It's as if every breath we breathe is longing for the One who pursues us. In every thought, we hope for more of Him. In every moment, we long to see Him, to touch Him, and to be in His presence. Our blood flows for Him, and with every heartbeat, we realize Jesus is the One who brings into our marriage the connection we desire with our spouse.

Think of it this way. Suppose I invite you and your spouse to join me onstage. I ask each of you to hold out one hand. I place your hands together as if you are cupping water and then cover your hands with a cloth. I ask you both to think of anything in the world. Simultaneously, you both think of the beach. Neither of you know that you are thinking of the same word. But as I snap my finger and whip away the cloth, you both hold sand between your fingers. Your spouse smiles, and you smile as a flood of incredible memories rushes through your mind. Your eyes water as you're reminded of your deep love for each other. Each of you carries some sand back with you to your seat as I continue the show. This experience of magic couldn't happen without the magician. Similarly, intimacy with each other is best experienced and understood through connection with the One who made us.

The best way to express intimacy with God is to share a few verses with you. Pray through these verses and ask God to bring you closer to Him. A byproduct of becoming closer to God is becoming closer to your spouse.

Ponder these verses.

Psalm 63:1 (ESV)

"O God, you are my God; earnestly I seek you;
my soul thirsts for you;

my flesh faints for you,
in a dry and weary land where there is no water."

Jeremiah 24:7

"I will give them a heart to know me, that I am the Lord. They will be my people, and I will be their God, for they will return to me with all their heart."

2 Chronicles 7:14–15

"If my people, who are called by my name, will humble themselves, and pray and seek my face and turn from their wicked ways, then will I hear from heaven, and I will forgive their sin and will heal their land. Now my eyes will be open and my ears attentive to the prayers offered in this place."

Mark 12:30

"Love the Lord your God with all your heart and with all your soul and with all your mind and with all your strength."

Growth

Next, I want to show you some of the most effective life-strategies for creating dramatic changes in your intimacy with God in the context of your marriage. God has incredible things in store for you. Yet God allows us to choose to pursue growth and intimacy with Him. He doesn't force His will on us but pursues us diligently until we respond to His invitation.

As you design a plan for growing in your faith, it will have a significant impact on your relationship with God and your marriage.

No recipe works for everyone, but the following are some of the best practices to foster growth in your relationship with God and with your spouse.

Asking and Sharing

Ask your spouse, "How are you growing in your faith?" Learning to have faith conversations is transformative for many marriages. As with most conversations in marriage, beginning with questions can open the door for powerful communication.

Tell your spouse about your faith journey. In sharing your story first, you're taking the initiative. Text a verse. Share an answered prayer. Talk about something you learned. As you develop these two habits—asking and sharing—you'll create an intimacy with each other that's centered on your relationship with God.

KIMBERLY'S CORNER

Don't forget to dream together. As I've mentioned, Danny is the dreamer and I tend to be the dream crusher. However, we wouldn't be writing this book if Danny and I hadn't talked about and dreamed about what it would look like if we were to one day put a book out there that might help people to have a stronger marriage.

Sometimes our dreams work out, and sometimes they don't. Sometimes one of you might have a dream that is a little too far out there, but together you can make it more realistic. Again, this is another opportunity to be Team Us. Go on coffee dates together and talk about where you want to be and what you want to be doing one year from now, five years from now, and twenty years from now. Dream together about work, family, friends, your home, vacations, and where you want to be in your walk with God.

Mentoring

Another catalyst for growth is to seek ways of being mentored. This can happen one-on-one, or you can join a small group that challenges you to live out your faith. There is power in having someone who is further along the path than you speak wisdom and encouragement into your life. If this is too much for you initially, listen to a podcast, an audiobook, or watch a YouTube video of someone who can teach you how to be more intimate with God. Check out *dannyraymarriage.com* for more ideas and resources. Having an actual mentor (or mentors) is life changing, so make it the goal and work toward finding one, even if you aren't ready to take that step today.

Encouragement

The phone can often lead to a thousand distractions (we talked about that in several chapters), but it's also an incredible tool to empower your spouse to become who God designed them to be. Kimberly and I have found that texting each other verses, prayers, and words of encouragement can deepen our relationship with God and with each other.

Solitude

Being silent is a lost art. We are constantly talking, moving, or listening to a million voices at once. In fact, it's hard to find a place where music isn't playing (the store, the elevator, the waiting room, the car) and where background noise is minimal. In our culture, people rarely create space in their schedules to be still and listen, let alone listen to God. Yet God tells us, "Be still, and know that I am God" (Psalm 46:10). To deepen our intimacy with God, we need to learn to be still, be silent, and listen to the lover of our souls.

These moments of solitude remind us of the person we are meant to be, which helps us to love our spouse more, to listen more intently, and to encourage their intimacy with God as well.

Passions

Find things that you love to do as a couple and individually. Dance? Watch football? Go to concerts? Sing? Play games? God is with us 24/7, waiting for us to awaken to His presence in everything. He created you to enjoy certain activities for a reason. Learning to draw close to God by following your passions will bring a joy that's not attainable any other way.

Car Trips

I could give you a hundred more ideas on how to grow in your intimacy with God and with each other but let me end with this one. We drive a lot in our culture. I'm constantly on the road for shows, and Kimberly and I drive to see friends and family, to hang out for a day in Hollywood, or to visit our boys while they are in school. Those miles in the car together provide an opportunity to listen to podcasts, sermons, or audiobooks that challenge us in our faith. How could you take advantage of car time with your spouse?

This isn't meant to be an exhaustive list, just a way to spur you toward action and to encourage you to live out your faith together.

Here are a few more just for fun:

- Buy a devotional from your favorite author and read it together.
- Study a character you've always loved in the Bible (e.g., David, Esther, Gideon, Peter, Paul, Ruth).
- Go to a movie and look for faith themes in the plot that the two of you can talk about (grace, redemption, hope, hypocrisy).
- Go surfing and think about God's love being higher, deeper, longer, wider than any ocean.
- Take an art class together.

- Play some games together and ask why God created laughter.
- Grab a $100 and give it away. Talk about how God gives to you.
- Pray in a place you have never prayed before.
- Pick an exercise and thank God for movement (even if it's bowling).

God's Plan

God has bigger plans for you. Seriously. His plans have been thought out over eternity. How often do you think about God's plan for your marriage? What does He want to do through the two of you together?

As you discover His plan, you'll experience God's blessing and favor. One of my core beliefs is that God has a better plan for our lives than we do. He has higher standards, bigger dreams, and a more fulfilling marriage for us than we could ever imagine.

As we trust in Him and His plan, we grow in our understanding of Him, we deepen our relationship with Him, and we experience the God-sized life that He has in store for us and our marriage.

As we grow in our intimacy with God, we will learn to view our marriage from God's perspective. We will see that God unlocks the fullness of our marriage.

My passion is to help couples move from where they are to where God wants them to be. The key is not to move there overnight but to daily head in that direction. To do this, we need to believe that God has bigger dreams for our marriage. As our intimacy with God increases, our marriage will align with His will.

God has designed your marriage for this moment, this space in time, this day, this life. Don't waste it. This is your time in history to love and honor your spouse. Make the most of every moment!

CREATING MAGIC TOGETHER

TAKEAWAY

The best way to understand each other is to understand how we are made. And the best way to do this is to understand our Creator. Knowing how God created marriage and intended it to flourish and bless those who enter into it is a huge step toward living your marriage to the fullest.

QUESTIONS

Ask each other: How close is your relationship with God on a scale of one to ten (one is distant; ten is close)? What's one activity we could do together to become closer to God?

PLAN OF ACTION

Create a plan to get away for a week or weekend, to get closer to God. Use that time to make God a greater part of your daily lives. If you have children, involve them in carrying out the plan, too. Help them learn how important it is to involve God in every aspect of life.

15

CREATING MAGIC TOGETHER

Enjoying a Grace-Filled Marriage

For from his fullness we have all received, grace upon grace.

—John 1:16

One of my favorite things about close-up magic is that it happens in the spectator's hands. Different from seeing an illusion from a distance, close-up magic increases the participant's astonishment because it seems so impossible that something could change inches from your face.

In many magic tricks, the outcome changes based on the spectator's decision. Usually, in these cases, when the magician fails to obtain the desired outcome that leads to the best effect (outcome A), he or she quickly goes with option B or C. The secondary outcomes are still good, but the magician knows it's not the best possible outcome.

In the past, when outcome B or C happened, I was discouraged because I know I can deliver a higher level of astonishment. However, in recent years, I've learned to give myself some grace. I need to make the most of the moment, because the audience experiencing B or C are enjoying the *only* outcome they'll experience together. In other words, even though I know the effect could be more astonishing, they laugh and clap because they've still seen something amazing.

Your marriage is more about grace than being right or wrong. If you're going to create magic together, you need a grace-filled life.

> Grace is undeserved.
>
> Grace is un-shuffling the chaos.
>
> Grace is contagious.
>
> Grace is the glue that holds marriages together.
>
> Grace is an ocean of yeses that chooses to never give up.
>
> Grace is radical.
>
> Grace is God's heart revealed.
>
> God is grace-filled. And because of His grace, we'll never be the same.

Grace changes us and moves us. Grace is what every marriage needs to thrive. Without it, we're doomed to judgment and to facing our ever-growing failures.

I love being married to the woman of my dreams. Kimberly and I are flawed. Occasionally, we still do foolish things, but there's so much grace and forgiveness in our marriage that I remember far more moments of grace than moments of shame. My wife paints Christ's grace in her actions, in her tone, and in every other way. She loves God and treats me as the man I am becoming, not the man I am.

Why is it so hard to show grace? I suppose it's because we don't have a category for it. We have a category for wrongs. We guard and protect ourselves so we won't get wronged again. But grace is vulnerable. Grace isn't safe. Grace could be stolen, abused, and lost. Grace is risky for the giver. Grace is also risky for the receiver. But grace isn't an option for followers of Christ. Grace should flow through our veins.

Grace is the gift God has freely given to us, and we need to give it freely to our spouses every day.

Reset

Kimberly and I often ask other couples, "What tools do you have in your toolbox?" In other words, what tools do you have to overcome suffering, to communicate with each other, to show grace. One of our tools is the Reset button. Now if this button were real, it would be worn down because we have pressed it so often.

Let me explain how the Reset button works in our marriage. Kimberly and I were driving to a friend's house. Thankfully, we have never had any fights in the car (yeah, right). As I was driving, someone cut me off. In my head, I knew I had been there before, so it was no big deal to give them a pass. But my wife saw this as a teachable moment. While I swerved out of the way, she reached across the car and slammed her hand on the horn and glared at the guy. Team Us forever, right!

At the time, I was frustrated by her actions. I was playing defense against the other car and defense against my wife. But my ninja skills only work with decks of cards, so the frustration of that moment led to an argument. Unlike a lot of fights that can be resolved by getting all the parties involved, together, this one was stuck. After all, if this person hadn't cut me off, Kimberly and I wouldn't be arguing, right? Maybe.

When we find ourselves in situations like that, we say, "Can I have a do-over?" or "Can I hit the Reset button?" In fact, these days we usually say, "Reset!" We know this means that the other person is asking for some grace, a chance to back up, and do their best to start over. One simple word has had an amazing impact on our marriage because it's a word that demands grace.

Gift Giving

Grace is defined as unmerited or undeserved favor. Grace is giving a gift to your spouse simply out of love. There are always opportunities to give freely to your spouse but also look for ways to give grace in a way that makes them feel loved.

In 2008, I traveled to Japan to do fourteen shows in twelve days. Kimberly and I were aware that the pressures on the road and at home would increase exponentially each day I was away. Because two full weeks would have been the longest trip I had experienced away from my family, I wanted to let my wife know, in a practical way, that I loved her, that I missed her, and that I was so thankful she was taking care of everything back home while I traveled. Before I left on the trip, I went down to our local UPS store and talked to the team there—back then I was seeing them at least three to five times a week. I asked, "If I leave twelve gifts with you, will you put one of them in our family's mailbox each day?"

They said, "We'll do better than that. We'll deliver one to your doorstep each day!"

This occurred long before Amazon's two-day delivery system, so it was an incredible surprise for Kimberly, and a great mystery, on how these gifts were arriving. The twelve gifts were a tangible way that I (along with my secret team) could give to my wife and make her feel loved, cherished, and appreciated.

She loved it. Each day she was surprised that there was yet another gift mysteriously showing up on the porch. The gifts made the days a little easier to bear, since she was taking care of three kids under the age of ten and was tired from the endless diaper changes and demands for constant attention. She told me later that those gifts were a rainbow in the storm.

There are always ways to give to your spouse in practical, unexpected ways. I'm always surprised and excited to find a love note from my wife, which she often adds to my suitcase before I head out of town to speak and perform.

KIMBERLY'S CORNER

The key to making magic in your marriage is giving grace and forgiveness. Every couple gets angry, and anger is not a sin. It's what you do when you're angry that can potentially be sinful, (e.g., yelling or name-calling). But the real magic is in the forgiveness and grace.

When you screw up or do something you know might upset your spouse, don't you already feel bad? You probably didn't mean to hurt them, but you did, so now what? Wouldn't it be amazing if your spouse said they were hurt by your actions, but they were working on forgiving you, and instead of yelling at you, they gave you a long embrace?

If you're thinking that would be something you would truly appreciate, then why not extend that same grace and forgiveness to your spouse the next time they make you mad? Instead of acting like you are so much better than they are and as if you would never make their mistake, assume the best in them. Forgive early and often. God grants us His grace and mercy all the time, so who are we to withhold that from our loved ones?

Giving consistently changes your marriage for the better. Here are two ways you can give today.

1. **Time and Attention**

   It's been said that love is spelled t-i-m-e. Giving your spouse your time is a precious gift. The gift of time should be uninterrupted and distraction free. Put down your cell phones, everyone, and turn off the TV.

2. **Talents**

   Maybe you're great at organizing, and you know your spouse wants something organized, like your closet or pile of receipts. Use your time and talents to bring them joy or at least help them out.

On my wrist I wear a watch Kimberly gave to me for our twenty-fifth wedding anniversary. I love it. It reminds me of her love for me all the time.

What about you? What could you give your spouse?

Let me share something my wife does well that shows grace in action. Sometimes, after a moment of tension, she'll leave the room and return with a chocolate chip cookie and a cup of coffee. She often does this after I haven't been at my best, but she definitely understands me, and she exemplifies grace in action.

What would be grace in action to your spouse? It may be something edible like a chocolate chip cookie. But it could very well be an act of service. Maybe you could prepare his favorite meal or take her to her favorite restaurant. Perhaps her love language is words, and you could write a love letter that she could read and reread. Think about some of the meaningful things you have done over the years and how your spouse reacted to them.

Creating Magic Together

On the silver screen, it's easy to see when a couple creates magic together. The chemistry is undeniable, even envious. Something about the way they treat each other and the way they laugh together sparks the magic. We root for them to overcome the impossible situations in which they find themselves. Like most intangibles, creating magic in marriage is hard to explain. It's like asking someone to describe color, the wind, or love. But you know it when you see it. And without a daily dispensing of grace, creating magic together will never happen.

CREATING MAGIC TOGETHER

TAKEAWAY

Grace is big part of creating magic together in marriage. Grace means giving what others don't deserve with no thought of something in return. Grace is what God gives us every day so we can give it to our spouse.

QUESTIONS

1. When was the last time your spouse showed you grace? How did it make you feel?
2. When was the last time you wished for some grace and didn't receive it? Discuss how that negative experience made you feel and how you could do better next time.
3. Think about all the grace God has given to you. How does that make you feel?

PLAN OF ACTION

God gives us limitless grace. Since His supply will never diminish, when you trust Him you will have access to all that grace in your relationship. For one week, think about every way you can shower your mate with grace. When you wake up, bring them coffee or breakfast in bed. Compliment them every day. Do a chore you don't normally do. Deflect any triggers instead of responding to them as usual. (New scripts!) Do something they love to do, that you don't. Be creative. Not only will you make their week, you might make yours too.

16

OVER THE TOP

Keeping the End in Mind

Now to him who is able to do immeasurably more than all we ask or imagine.

—Ephesians 3:20

One of the things I love about the art of magic is show structure. For me, designing a show from beginning to end is never a linear process. I always start with the end: Do I want their jaws to drop open? Do I want the audience silent, shocked, or maybe inspired? One show I designed ended with an underwater escape. The question I left the audience with was this: "When you take your final breath, who will you be?" Everything in the show led to that final moment. When I defined where I was going, I developed a show to fit that purpose.

Structure

To better understand how you can create magic in your marriage, I want to dive into show structure. This concept doesn't apply only to a magic show but also to a great concert, the best movies, good books, and as you will see, our marriages.

Let's say you're watching a show with no build up, no drama, and no tension. The show becomes like a boring lecture. See the diagram below.

Beginning. **The End.**

The linear structure makes it hard for the audience to stay engaged.

Most people think their favorite shows are more like the following diagram. The writing seems to get better and better, and the audience is never bored. But that's not true. No show can sustain complete upward trajectory.

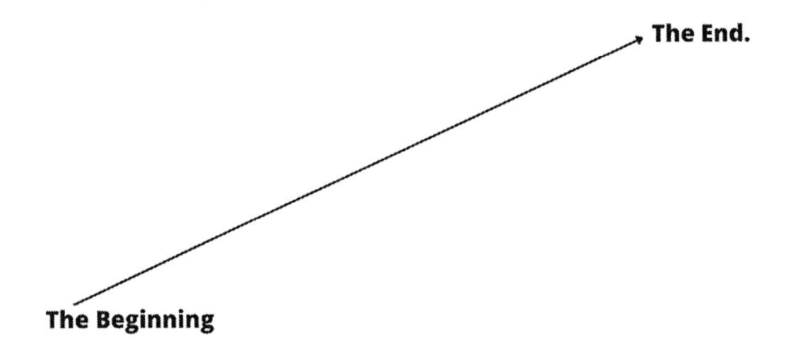

The following is a better depiction of how a great show builds. Week after week, it keeps getting better and better, but the program also gives you less dramatic moments to process, reflect, or simply enjoy parts of the plot. When you're caught up in the story again, the character development gets more interesting, then the show plateaus for a few moments before it comes to an incredible conclusion. The buildup is fantastic!

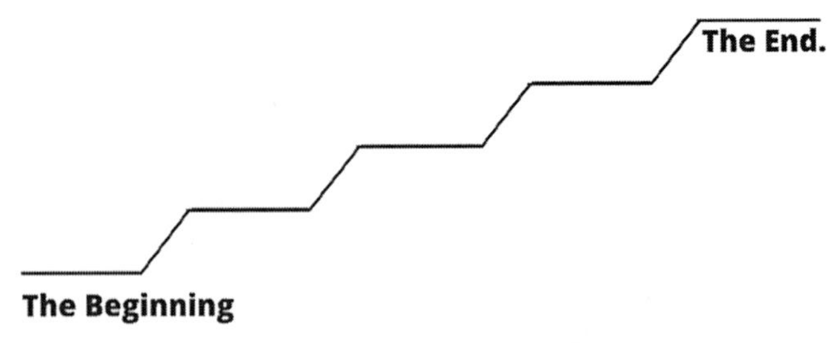

Sometimes we think our marriages are more like a linear journey, but God's plan for you and your spouse is to grow closer, love each other more, and over time, watch your relationship become better and better.

Keeping the end in mind, ask yourself these questions: Where is your marriage going? Where do you want it to go?

The beauty of reading those questions right now is that if there is a gap, if there is a difference between where you want to go and where you headed right now, you have time to close that gap and get your marriage on track. Maybe the gap between the goal and the reality seems too great. You want a marriage that is thriving and filled with joy. But you can't picture it. I encourage you with a reminder: nothing is impossible with God.

We look at our marriages—the struggle, the pain, the suffering, the brokenness—and it's hard for us to wrap our minds around the fact that none of these obstacles can keep God from doing what He is able to do. We see impossible situations every day, but God has never looked at any marriage and thought that He had finally found one that is impossible to

KIMBERLY'S CORNER

Danny definitely brings my life over the top. I would hate to think of my life without him, but if I had lived my life on my own, I would have missed so many over-the-top moments and a lot of crazy adventures.

A safe, average life would have been fine with me if I never knew what I was missing, but having lived these twenty-five years married to Danny, I have seen and done some crazy, somewhat impossible things. I've taken trips I never would have chosen on my own—chased sunrises, ridden a zodiac boat way too fast, slept next to a beehive in a 100-year-old house, and helped write a book.

Through all the adventures, God has grown me and stretched me, and I am thankful. Keep the end in mind and focus on the joy you can create along the way as a team.

fix. He has never looked at someone suffering and thought He couldn't help them or didn't know how to make them well. God always has a way to do the impossible.

The word *impossible* does not exist in God's vocabulary. He's in the business of doing the impossible in our lives. The question for us is, are we willing to allow God to do the impossible in our marriage? Even if you have a partner who doesn't want to improve things right now, you can still end up with a great marriage. You do what you can right now. Start praying for your marriage, start pouring grace into your spouse. Even though marriage is a team sport, one person can hold up the team for a season and move toward a great marriage. Your commitment shows your spouse that you are on their side even through difficult seasons.

Over the Top

Maybe your marriage is getting better and better and is heading in the right direction. I challenge you to make it an over-the-top marriage. Let me explain.

I love creating moments that seem impossible. A playing card appears in a sealed pack of gum. A random number leads to a specific prediction. A thought or word appears in a spectator's hands.

These astonishing moments create wonder, but in the context of a show, I can build toward an incredible ending. I love to keep the momentum going from one trick to the next. I keep building until the audience explodes in applause, sometimes leaping to their feet or literally falling out of their seats as I finish my final piece. As a magician and a performer, I want to create an over-the-top experience.

I've built my show with the end in mind, and the audience believes that the show is over, and they loved it. This is where I have spent thousands of hours in show creation. If the show has ended in their minds, and I do one more trick that is a complete surprise—one that is better than anything else I have done all night—I will have created the most magical experience possible.

What if we could do this in our marriages? You ask your wife on a date and instead of getting in your car, you pick her up in her favorite car—a lime-green 1972 Pinto. You drive up a hill to your favorite spot to watch the sunset while eating tacos. (If she's on a health kick, you're eating kale tacos with cabbage and tofu). After dancing in the dark and experiencing lots of laughs, you tell her you have a final surprise. You coast down the hill listening to your favorite tunes until you arrive at her favorite ice cream shop. (If she is still on a health kick, insert water and ice here). On your way home, when she thinks the date night is over, you drive to a hotel, and she discovers you have packed an overnight bag and covered the details for childcare too! (Next-level surprise: A weekend away? A flight to her favorite destination?)

The point isn't about the money you spend, it's about continually creating unexpected experiences that build up your spouse. Over-the-top moments let them know that you are thinking about them even when you are not with them.

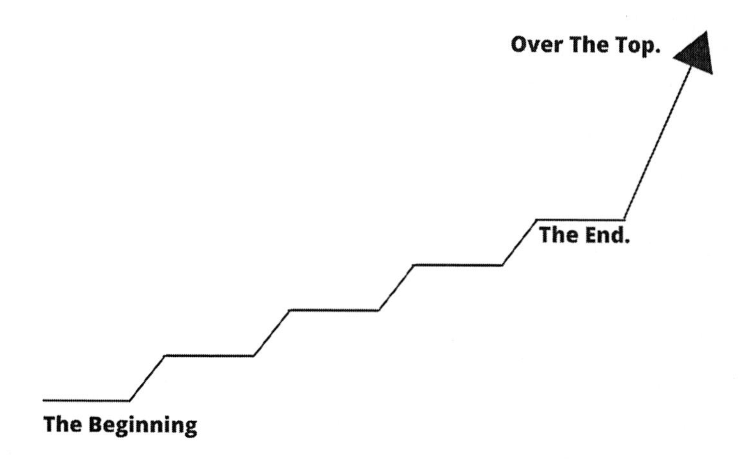

Commitment

When I do a show, I'm committed to creating an over-the-top moment at some point in the night. It doesn't always happen, and sometimes it happens in unexpected ways. One time I was doing a show and the cutest kid in the world wandered onto the stage. The auditorium was packed with a thousand plus people. I thought, whose kid is this? Get him back to his parents, and let's continue with the rest of the show. However, I said, "Hi, there." He waved, and the audience went nuts laughing and clapping. I jumped right in and did something completely unplanned with this kid that turned out to be the highlight of the show. It was my over-the-top moment. Like I said, it doesn't always happen, but I'm always striving for that kind of a show. Incidentally, I've done numerous shows where a marriage proposal is planned as part of the show. When the guy bends on one knee, it is always an over-the-top moment.

In your marriage, you need to commit to do whatever it takes to create magic. You'll have plenty of over-the-top moments that are unplanned, but you have the opportunity to commit to and plan some over-the-top moments. You can't do that every day, but you can make a birthday, an anniversary, a Christmas, or a special date an over-the-top experience.

Ten Thousand Kisses

People ask how I create a brand-new magic trick. The process is hard to explain. When I created my ring-in-light-bulb routine, I stared at a light bulb, hours upon hours, dreaming up the craziest trick I could possibly do with it. When I developed my version of a famous trick called Any Card at Any Number, my first thought was big: what if I did this trick with a million playing cards instead of fifty-two? I didn't hit my goal of a million playing cards, which is over nineteen thousand decks of cards. I performed the trick with roughly ten thousand playing cards, though, and created an incredible image, which made that variation uniquely mine.

You write the story of your marriage. Maybe you take one idea and run with it. Maybe create your own. Whatever you do, I'd love to hear your stories.

Let me throw out some ideas and then you figure out ways to go over-the-top in your marriage.

- One thousand kisses in one hundred cities—that's ten thousand delicious smooches!
- Four cars, three planes, two boats, one bike. Go!
- One hundred sunsets, one drink, seven keys, and a treasure
- Mountains, beach, no car in twenty-three and half hours
- Exotic location, Danny Ray event, amazement
- Ten watches, no wallet, one telescope
- One thousand candles, two wineglasses, apple pie

Okay, it's your turn. What's the start of something the two of you could plan together to create an epic over-the-top story?

CREATING MAGIC TOGETHER

TAKEAWAY

And over-the-top marriage requires a commitment to engaging your spouse in meaningful ways. You can create amazing, unforgettable, and beautiful moments by always being a student of the person you married.

QUESTIONS

1. At your funeral, what do you want people to say about our marriage?
2. What can we do to better live out our purpose?

PLAN OF ACTION

1. Plan a date night that you can do in the next seven days. Ask your spouse out for the date and only tell them the time and how to dress.
2. Plan an over-the-top experience you can do in the next six months. Keep building the suspense on this one. Drop hints or reminders.

17

HOUSE OF CARDS

Creating A Legacy-Driven Marriage

We will not hide them from their children, but tell to the coming generation the glorious deeds of the Lord, and his might, and the wonders that he has done.

—Psalm 78:4 (ESV)

A house of cards is always built on the right foundation. But even if the foundation is solid, building a house of cards is a delicate operation; taking one card out can send the whole structure crumbling to the ground. Our marriages are fragile, too, and we need to handle them with care every day.

We don't want to go through the motions of life and settle for a mediocre marriage. We want to build a marriage that is filled with love, laughter, and hope. We want a marriage that thrives and empowers others to live fully. Leaving a marriage legacy isn't about your life becoming a household name. It's about doing the most you can with what God has given you. If you're going to have a legacy-driven marriage, decide what you want to leave behind and go after that in small ways every day. Legacy is about how you live, not what you give. It's your life that eventually tips the scale toward massive impact.

KIMBERLY'S CORNER

Life is short. Make your marriage count. Choose to forgive. Admit your mistakes and learn to laugh at them. Let your children or family members see how you work together as a team and inspire other married couples to do the same.

What do you want your kids to take from watching your marriage and apply to their own? Don't go to bed angry. Start each day on the same page with your spouse. If something is bothering you, talk about it. Don't be selfish. Figure out what you can do to show your love to your spouse so that they know you care and that you are for them, not against them.

These are not huge things, but they make an incredible difference here and in eternity.

Legacy-Driven

Legacy became important to me the day my daughter, Caroline, was born. As she traveled from the womb to the doctor's hands, she swallowed fluid, making it difficult for her lungs to function. As a daddy, your heart races with every unknown medical issue your child encounters.

The doctor called in a team of nurses, who surrounded Caroline. One held an oxygen mask to her tiny newborn face. Other nurses drew blood. Everything happened so fast. The medical team rushed her down the hallway, and I followed close behind, glancing back at Kimberly, who was in tears but telling me to go. The team moved behind a glass wall doing everything they could to make sure Caroline had everything she needed to live. Eventually, the doctor invited me in and said, "Our Neonatal Care Unit is completely full. We've called two other hospitals. The only hospital that has room for your daughter is twenty-five miles away. She'll be taken in an ambulance immediately. You can meet the team over there."

I wasn't going to let Caroline out of my sight, so I asked my mom to let Kimberly know what was going on as I rushed to my car. Through my tears, I followed the ambulance, and that trip taught me a life-lesson I'll never forget: life is fragile. I spent the next two days at the hospital in a chair by Caroline's side—as much time as the staff let me. Kimberly eventually joined me for an eleven-day journey in the NICU. I had lots of time to think about the stories I wanted Caroline to hear growing up. What kind of father will she remember? What kind of husband do I want to become for the sake of my daughter? What legacy will I leave behind, not only for my children but also for neighbors, coworkers, and friends? Life passes so quickly. Life is so fragile.

What are we doing with our marriages that matters?

Carpe Diem

Today is the only day we've been given to love our spouses, to create over-the-top moments, to show grace, and to be the best spouse we can possibly be. Today is where legacies are created.

You stand on the shoulders of kings, teachers, innovators, leaders, and generations of other people who chose to have extraordinary marriages. History is full of real-life love stories; books, movies, and television are filled with true-love stories. We are drawn to them. Together, you and your spouse get to decide what type of story you live.

Creating a legacy-driven marriage requires small steps, one after another, in the right direction, beginning now.

In the movie *Dead Poets Society*, John Keating—a maverick teacher—turns toward glass cases filled with trophies, footballs, and team pictures. As the students slowly gather around the cases, they see the memorabilia of days gone by. Keating looks at his students as they gaze into the forgotten faces and stories of students from another era. Then he challenges them with these words:

> They're not that different from you, are they? Same haircuts. Full of hormones, exactly like you. Invincible, just like you

> feel. The world is their oyster. They believe they're destined for great things, also like many of you. Their eyes are full of hope, just like you. Did they wait until it was too late to make from their lives even one iota of what they were capable? Because, you see gentlemen, these boys are now fertilizing daffodils. But if you listen real close, you can hear them whisper their legacy to you. Go on, lean in. Listen, you hear it? *Carpe*—hear it?—*Carpe, carpe diem.* Seize the day boys. Make your lives extraordinary.[10]

Now, it's your turn to seize the day. This is your chance to make this life extraordinary, and you don't have time to waste. One day, you too will be an image behind a trophy case, and others will lean in to hear your story. So make your story great! Listen carefully to those who have gone before you, and hear them say, "*Carpe diem, carpe diem.* Seize the day. Make your life extraordinary."

I say to you, *carpe diem.* Make your marriage extraordinary!

Dramatically Improve Your Marriage

One amazing insight can improve your marriage in significant ways. If you implement this strategy, you will create magic in your marriage like never before. This three-part system for creating magic is all about increasing intimacy in your marriage, not only in the bedroom but also by learning that intimacy is sharing all of your life with your best friend.

1. Increase the frequency of your intimacy.
2. Increase the depth of your intimacy.
3. Increase the length of time of your intimacy.

We can't live every moment at a deep, intimate level. However, we can all look for opportunities to increase how often, how deep, and how long we choose to be intimate with each other. Intimacy doesn't automatically happen in the bedroom. Intimacy happens in conversations, in serving each other, and in experiencing life's adventures together. If you make an increase in one of these areas, you'll experience growth in your marriage. If you both intentionally go after growth in all three of these areas, you'll experience a tremendous amount of fulfillment in your marriage. Intimacy matters. You were designed for a deep, meaningful marriage. Time spent investing in your intimacy, is time well spent!

Hit the Ground Running

Every morning in Africa, a gazelle wakes up.

It knows it must outrun the fastest lion or it will be killed.

Every morning in Africa, a lion wakes up.

It knows that it must run faster than the slowest gazelle, or it will starve.

It doesn't matter whether you're a lion or a gazelle

when the sun comes up you'd better be running.[11]

Can you imagine how your marriage would change if you woke up with that kind of passion every day? What would be different if you loved your spouse as if your life depended on it? You would approach creating a legacy-driven marriage with passionate pursuit.

The key is this: you must know what you need to run from and what you need to run after. What you run from and what you run toward, more than anything else, will determine the person you become. Running with purpose and passion will be part of your legacy.

Grab a piece of paper and draw a line right down the center. Think about your marriage and then write a list of the things you need to run from on right side and a list of things you need run after on the left side.

Here are some examples from my own life.

RUNNING FROM	RUNNING TOWARD
Staying up late and letting my wife go to bed on her own	Plan on going to bed together
Forgetting date night because of busy schedule	Planning date night and putting it on the calendar
Distractions	Focusing on my wife and listening to her
Not encouraging	Empowering, encouraging, speaking life into my wife
Forgetting to ask about her hopes and dreams	Helping her to become the person God has designed her to be
Being too busy	Carving out time to enjoy life together

Okay, your turn. Make a list. Pick one pair of running-from and running-toward statements and choose to put it into practice immediately. Intensity fades if we don't immediately put into practice what we learn, so make a commitment to run both away from and toward something today.

CREATING MAGIC TOGETHER

TAKEAWAY

In our marriages, we have patterns and paths that we must leave behind so that we can run toward the goals we want to achieve, and the legacies we want to leave. Now is the perfect time to change course.

QUESTIONS

1. Seize the day. How does that phrase apply to you and your marriage? How can you make the most of your marriage every day?
2. What are you running from in your marriage? What should you be running toward?

PLAN OF ACTION

Talk about the legacy you want to leave for your family. What are the three most important things you want your children or close loved ones to take away from watching you and your spouse live and love together? What can you change today to make that happen?

Find couples who have great marriages. I challenge you to find at least three. Ask them their best advice for having a great marriage. Make a list of the things you learn. Discuss how you can implement them or adjust them to help you make your marriage even stronger.

18

THE GRAND FINALE

San Diego. Lights. Five thousand Seats. Sold out. Posters reading "Experience a sensational underwater escape by world renowned illusionist, Danny Ray. Failure to escape means death."

Standing under the bright lights, I heard the metal container being filled behind me as several audience members examined multiple handcuffs from different eras, including a modern pair. I asked for the strongest man in the room and shackled him with a Darby set of handcuffs. I then asked him to attempt to break free. He pulled and wedged a knee in between each cuff to attempt to break out. He couldn't. I even gave him the keys and let him try, but he still couldn't remove the cuffs. Darby's are, by far, the most difficult set of cuffs from which to escape. After the man's many attempts to remove the cuffs, I inserted the key, twisting it several times before the cuffs released.

Next, I presented six massive locks and passed them out to different audience members. "Please examine the locks and make sure they are exactly what they appear to be."

Someone called out, "Where is the key so I can test it."

"Sir, come up here," I said. When I handed him the key, I added, "You probably want to check out the metal container as well."

"Well, okay," he said. "This lock works, and yes, I will check out this contraption." He pulled and pushed on every part of the container. At one point he dipped his arm into the container and, as he felt around, the audience giggled and murmured that the guy wasn't going to let me get away with anything.

After he was satisfied that what he was about to see would be an actual escape, he took a seat to the applause of an audience. The audience loved the fact that one of their own got to examine everything.

At this time, I stepped to center stage and said, "In a moment, I'm going to be shackled and submerged underwater. Six locks will ensure that it's impossible for me to escape, yet that's exactly what I will attempt to do—the impossible. Eventually, we're all going to take our last breath. As I go underwater, I want you to hold your breath with me, and if at some point you let out your air, I want you to think about this: where are you going to be when you take your last breath?"

At that point in my career, I was able to hold my breath for four minutes. Most people can't hold their breath for one minute, which meant that in less than a minute after I went underwater, the question about taking our last breath was circling through each audience member's mind.

As I finished talking, an audience member locked me into the handcuffs and made sure they were secure. Jeremiah, my assistant, had collected the locks and was ready to secure the lid to what could become my metal coffin. As I stepped into the container, water spilled out. I looked upward and took slow, methodical, deep breaths. (All my training goes into that moment because it requires complete focus.)

The music was playing so loud I could feel it in my chest, but as I took deeper and deeper breaths, I felt almost like I wasn't there. Almost like there was no audience. Just me and God.

My prayer during this escape routine is always the same: *God, this is for You. May You be glorified. May this help people, maybe just one person, choose to live intentionally.*

I took slow breaths as I completely immersed myself under the water. Above me, the lid snapped into place. The timer in my head started—one second, two, three.

00:17

The locks around the tank clicked as Jeremiah secured them—one, two, three, four, five, six.

00:54

I found the pick hidden in my watch and started working systematically on each cuff.

01:07

First, I determined the order in which the cuffs were placed on me.

01:43

Next, the direction that each cuff was placed in became critical to unlocking them. Always working from the wrist up, I knew that if I had to break my thumbs to escape out of one of the cuffs, it would be easier with the cuffs closer to the elbow than to the wrist.

02:31

Just like I had done a thousand times before in rehearsals and on stage, I got out of each cuff.

By that time, everyone in the audience had stopped trying to hold their breath. On the edge of their seat, they wondered if I would make it out alive. Even my trusted assistant paced back and forth.

03:38

I made my way into the final part of the escape—an absolute mind bender because it would appear that I had melted through the container.

I had been in the container much longer than ever before. Underwater, I never check my watch. There is something absolutely terrifying about knowing how long you are underwater, knowing that you could drown. If I checked the time, I would lose 100 percent of my focus, and focus is essential for the illusion to go right.

That night, I felt like I had been locked up for about two minutes, which is how long it usually takes to get out.

> 04:34
>
> The curtain goes up and around the chamber of water for a moment, then immediately falls to the ground.
>
> 04:37
>
> I stood, hands raised in the air, dangling handcuffs clearly visible. Four minutes, thirty-seven seconds.
>
> The audience stood and applauded as I took a microphone and said, "Every breath you take matters. Thank you. Good night."

I stood in the back of the stadium that night, greeting thousands of people as they exited the event. A group of seven or eight people came by and said, "We know how you did it." I was kind of shocked because I work with a group of legendary underground escapologists who are the best in the world, and nobody—and I mean nobody—knows their secrets. One of these legends designed this piece, and there is no way in the world someone, even someone extremely knowledgeable in escapes, would have any clue about the intricate escape that the legendary escape artist designed for me. So, I was curious about what this group of people would say.

"We were at the very top of the stadium, and we could see over the curtain." A couple other of these college students chimed in: "Yeah man, we saw it all! We know how you did it."

I regret not thinking through those extreme sight lines because keeping this piece a mystery is important to me. But I asked, "What did you see?"

Understand that their response was seven people trying to explain everything all at once.

"Well, the curtain came up."

"Yeah, when it came up, we saw you."

"Yeah, we saw you. You came up."

"Then you went down."

"Then you came up, but this time you were holding the handcuffs."

"Yeah, we were like where did those come from."

"Wait, where did he come from?"

"Yeah, he was in the container. Then he wasn't. How did that happen, bro?"

"I don't know. I just know what I saw. He wasn't there, then he was there. Then he was there again, but he had handcuffs."

"Yeah, but how did he get out?"

"I don't know. He just appeared, but I saw it. He wasn't and then he was."

"But how?

"You were there. You saw. We know how you did it. It was amazing, though."

I thanked them for that incredibly detailed explanation as they headed out.

Combinations and Locks

I started training for escapes when I was fourteen years old. I had no idea how many locks, handcuffs, and keys my hands would handle over the years. But what I know is this: every lock has a combination or a key that unlocks it. If you forget the combination, you have to use secret underground methods, known by only a few experts, to unlock

KIMBERLY'S CORNER

This is a great time to think about the day you and your spouse said, "I do." You became Team Us forever. Teammates support, encourage, and trust each other.

Being vulnerable requires a lot of trust, which is vital in a marriage. When your spouse hurts you, your natural reaction might be to lash out. Instead, try telling them that they hurt your feelings without accusing or blaming them. Sharing your vulnerability and hurt can often turn things around. This is your teammate, so you don't want to hurt them because it will only hurt you as well. A helpful hint is to try to assume that your spouse didn't mean to hurt you. Assume the best in each other rather than the worst.

it. And if you lose the key, you need to learn methods to pick it open, assuming you don't want to destroy it by using bolt cutters.

Every lock is different, but they all have similarities as well. There are millions of locks, but only one key will unlock each of them. In other words, every lock has a perfect match. You are the perfect match for your spouse. Together you are Team Us. The marriage doesn't exist without both of you. Together you unlock the goodness of God's grace in your lives in ways that you could never do on your own.

To help us unlock the magic in our marriage, Kimberly and I found this verse: "In your anger do not sin: Do not let the sun go down while you are still angry" (Ephesians 4:26). Seriously, this verse has changed the trajectory of our marriage. It's as if God gave us a key to creating a magical marriage. From day one, we made a choice to not go to bed angry. Of the almost ten thousand days we've been married, there have been less than ten that we went to bed angry. The few days we did go to bed angry, we woke up the next morning and worked it out immediately. Being on the same page with my best friend every day creates magic in every area of our lives, but especially our marriage.

What Are the Odds?

What are the odds that you apply the principles in this book? That's your choice. You can read the book and say, "I'll highlight all the things my spouse should be doing." Or you can choose to make the small changes found throughout this book to make yourself into a better friend, a better lover, and a better spouse.

Every Breath You Take

Every breath we take is a gift of God. Our marriages can be magical, but we have to choose daily to say, "I want to use my breath, today, to love my spouse. No matter what happens, it's Team Us forever." We waste our breath and hurt our spouse when we use it to tear them down.

Check Everything Often and Always

I check each handcuff often—before I go on stage, during the show, and while I'm underwater. Failure to plan could end up with a failed attempt like I described at the beginning of this book. Even worse, it could result in serious injury or death.

The key in your marriage is to check it often and always make sure that you and your spouse are on the same page. When something doesn't check out, make the adjustments until you both are ready to move forward.

The Magic Team

Needless to say, the underwater escape never would have happened without Jeremiah in my corner. He was my secret weapon. He was the one I could count on. He knew everything necessary to keep me safe. He knew how everything worked and what to do if anything went wrong.

All of us need people cheering us on, people that help keep our marriage on course. We need at least one couple we can trust that will be in our corner praying for us, encouraging and challenging us to create the best marriage possible.

If you don't have someone you both can go to, pray that God will reveal a couple who can help you create a great marriage.

Create Magic Together

That final moment when I appear holding the handcuffs and the chamber still has six locks sealing it shut is truly magical. Breathtaking.

As you create magic in your marriage, you will be a blessing to many people around you. You choose your story, your way of creating magic in your marriage. No matter what season you're in, with God's help you can create a magical marriage.

Endnotes

[1] "Better to Remain Silent and Be Thought a Fool Than to Speak and Remove All Doubt," Quote Investigator, accessed September 6, 2021, https://quoteinvestigator.com/2010/05/17/remain-silent/.

[2] "4550.sapros," Bible Hub, accessed September 6, 2021, https://biblehub.com/greek/4550.htm.

[3] "Compassion," Etymonline, accessed September 6, 2021, https://www.etymonline.com/search?q=compassion.

[4] Sal Raichbach

[5] "Surprising Social Media Statistics—the 2021 Edition, Broadband Search, accessed September 6, 2021, https://www.broadbandsearch.net/blog/social-media-facts-statistics#post-navigation-0.

[6] "Comparison Is the Thief of Joy," Quote Investigator, accessed September 6, 2021, https://quoteinvestigator.com/2021/02/06/thief-of-joy/.

[7] "Internet Pornography by the Numbers; A Significant Threat to Society," Webroot, accessed September 6, 2021, https://www.webroot.com/us/en/resources/tips-articles/internet-pornography-by-the-numbers.

[8] "Oscar Wilde Quotes," BrainyQuote, accessed September 6, 2021, https://www.brainyquote.com/quotes/oscar_wilde_135813.

[9] "5281.hypomone," Bible Hub, accessed September 6, 2021, https://biblehub.com/greek/hypomone_s_5281.htm.

[10] Dead Poets Society, directed by Peter Weir, starring Robin Williams, Robert Sean Leonard, and Ethan Hawke (Burbank, CA: Touchstone Pictures, 1989).

[11] "The Fable of the Lion and the Gazelle," Quote Investigator, accessed September 6, 2021, https://quoteinvestigator.com/2011/08/05/lion-gazelle/.